THE GLOSSARY OF VISUAL DESIGN

Rhythm

Independent Publication

The Glossary of Visual Design

First Worldwide Edition

Complied & Edited by:
Manasi Pathak, Damayanti Jena

ISBN: 9798860394889

Published by:
Rhythm Independent Publication,
Jinkethimmanahalli, Varanasi, Bengaluru, Karnataka, India - 560036

For all types of correspondence, send your mails to the provided address above.

The information presented herein has been collated from a diverse range of sources, ensuring a comprehensive perspective on the subject matter.

Table of Contents

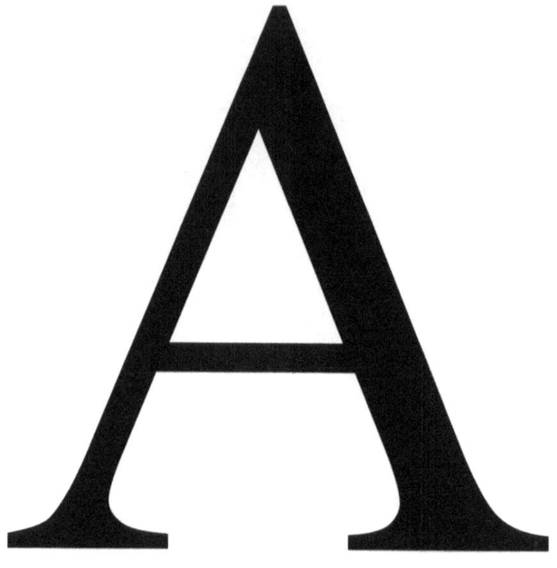

Alignment Consistency

Alignment Consistency, in the context of Design and User-Experience disciplines, refers to the practice of maintaining a consistent visual alignment throughout a design or user interface. It involves ensuring that all elements within a layout are properly aligned with one another, creating a harmonious and balanced composition.

Consistent alignment helps users understand the structure and hierarchy of information and interactions within a design. It establishes a visual rhythm that guides users' attention and aids in the efficient processing of content. When alignment is inconsistent, it can lead to confusion, visual clutter, and a subpar user experience.

Alignment Continuation

Alignment is a fundamental principle in both design and user experience disciplines. It refers to the arrangement of elements in a design or interface, creating a visual balance and cohesion. When elements are positioned in a way that they relate to one another and form a unified whole, they become more visually pleasing and easier for users to understand.

In design, alignment is crucial for organizing and structuring information. It helps create a clear hierarchy of elements, guiding users' attention and allowing them to navigate through the content effortlessly. By aligning elements such as text, images, and buttons, designers can establish a logical flow and prevent visual clutter.

Alignment Guides

Alignment guides in the context of design and user-experience disciplines refer to visual cues or guides that help designers and developers maintain consistent spacing, positioning, and alignment of elements. These guides ensure visual harmony, balance, and clarity in the overall design and also enhance the user experience.

Alignment plays a crucial role in design as it creates a sense of order and structure. It helps users understand the hierarchy of content, navigate through interfaces, and locate specific information or actions easily. By aligning elements such as text, images, buttons, and margins, designers establish a logical flow and establish a visual relationship between different elements.

Alignment Precision

Alignment Precision refers to the careful and deliberate arrangement of visual elements in a design or user experience in order to establish a sense of order, hierarchy, and balance. It involves ensuring that these elements are placed in a way that communicates a clear and cohesive message to the user.

In the context of design, alignment precision requires attention to detail and a keen eye for visual composition. It involves aligning elements such as text, images, and buttons in a way that creates balance and visual harmony. This can be achieved by using a grid system, where elements are placed along specific lines or columns, or by simply aligning elements based on their edges or centers.

In terms of user experience, alignment precision plays a crucial role in guiding the user's attention and helping them navigate through the interface. When elements are aligned properly, users can more easily understand the hierarchy of information, find what they are looking for, and complete tasks efficiently. On the other hand, poor alignment can create confusion and frustration for users, leading to a negative experience.

Overall, alignment precision is an essential aspect of design and user experience that contributes to the overall aesthetics, functionality, and usability of a product or interface. It requires careful consideration of the relationships between visual elements and the deliberate placement of these elements to create a visually appealing and intuitive experience.

Alignment Proximity

Alignment proximity is a principle in design and user-experience disciplines that refers to the way elements are visually connected or grouped together based on their alignment. It involves placing related elements in close proximity and aligning them along a consistent visual axis to create a sense of unity and organization.

By organizing elements using alignment proximity, designers can establish visual hierarchies, direct the user's attention, and enhance the overall user experience. When elements are aligned, they form a cohesive and structured layout, making it easier for users to scan and understand the content without confusion or cognitive effort.

Alignment Variation

Alignment variation in the context of design and user-experience disciplines refers to the deliberate arrangement and positioning of elements within a design or interface. It involves the strategic placement of elements to create balance, hierarchy, and visual cohesion.

Alignment plays a crucial role in guiding users' attention, enhancing readability, and facilitating efficient interactions. By aligning elements, designers create order and structure, making it easier for users to understand and navigate through the interface. It also helps convey the intended message and establish visual harmony.

Alignment

Alignment is a fundamental principle in design and user experience disciplines that refers to the placement and arrangement of visual elements in relation to each other and to the overall layout. It involves ensuring that elements are logically and visually connected, creating a cohesive and balanced design that is easy for users to understand and navigate.

Alignment, when effectively implemented, helps to establish a visual hierarchy, guiding users' attention and enabling them to quickly grasp the structure and meaning of the interface. It provides a sense of order and coherence, making the design visually appealing and enhancing user engagement and comprehension.

Analogous Colors

Analogous colors, in the context of design and user experience, refer to a set of colors that are closely related and sit next to each other on the color wheel. These colors are harmonious and often create a sense of unity and cohesion in a design.

When designing interfaces or websites, selecting analogous colors can be helpful in creating a visually pleasing and balanced composition. By using colors from the same color family, designers can easily create aesthetically pleasing designs that are easy on the eyes and create a sense of consistency.

Asymmetry

Asymmetry, in the context of design and user experience disciplines, refers to the intentional lack of balance or symmetry in the visual elements and layout of a design. It involves purposely deviating from the traditional principles of balance and harmony to create a sense of visual interest and unpredictability.

When applied in design, asymmetry can add dynamism and energy to a composition. It allows designers to create unique and memorable experiences by breaking away from predictable and uniform layouts. By introducing imbalance, designers can draw attention to specific elements, provoke emotions, and guide users through a design in a deliberate manner.

B

Broken Grid Layouts

A broken grid layout is a design approach that intentionally disrupts the traditional grid system used in graphic design and user experience disciplines. It deviates from the standard alignment of elements, such as text, images, and navigation items, to create a more dynamic and visually engaging layout.

Instead of adhering to a rigid grid structure based on columns and rows, a broken grid layout allows for asymmetry and irregularity. Elements are positioned in unexpected ways, overlapping or intersecting with one another, and breaking free from the constraints of a traditional grid.

Brand experience

Brand experience is a concept that is highly valued in both the design and user-experience disciplines. It refers to the overall perception and emotions that users have when interacting with a particular brand. This encompasses every touchpoint and interaction a user has with the brand, whether it's through a website, a mobile app, a physical store, customer service, or any other form of brand communication.

Brand experience is crucial because it can greatly influence a user's decision to engage with a brand, make a purchase, or become a loyal customer. When the experience is positive and memorable, it can create a strong emotional connection between the user and the brand, leading to increased trust and brand loyalty.

Branding strategy

A branding strategy in the context of design and user experience disciplines refers to a plan or approach adopted by a company or organization to establish and build its brand identity in the minds of its target audience. This strategy encompasses a set of actions and guidelines that aim to create a unique and consistent brand image, message, and perception across all touchpoints and interactions with the brand.

Design plays a pivotal role in shaping the brand strategy as it involves the visual representation and presentation of the brand to the audience. From the logo and typography to the color palette and overall aesthetics, the design elements need to align with the intended brand image and persona. Additionally, user experience (UX) plays a crucial role in brand strategy as it focuses on enhancing the users' interaction and perception of the brand through various touchpoints like websites, applications, and physical products.

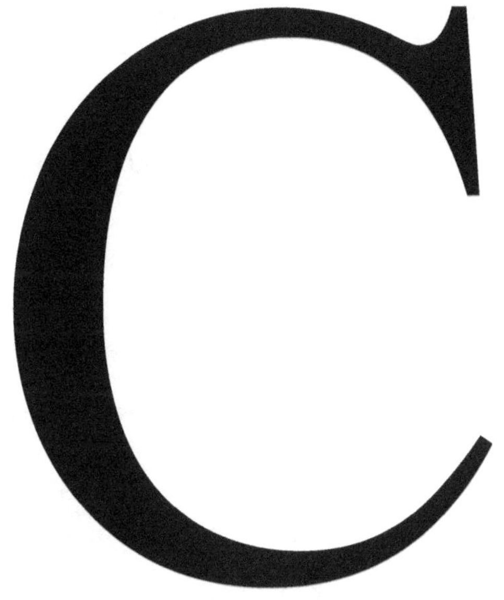

Card Design

A card design refers to a user interface element commonly used in the design and user experience disciplines. It is a visual representation of a piece of content or information, typically displayed as a rectangular box with some sort of shadow or border to give it depth and make it stand out from its surroundings.

Card designs are used to organize and present various types of content in a concise and user-friendly manner. They enable designers to create visually appealing and easily scannable layouts that help users quickly understand and interact with the information at hand.

These design elements often contain a combination of text, images, and interactive elements such as buttons or links. They are versatile and can be applied to a wide range of content, including articles, products, profiles, and media items.

Card designs are particularly popular in mobile app and responsive web design, as they offer a consistent and compact way of displaying information across different screen sizes and devices. They are also highly adaptable, as their modular nature allows for easy rearrangement and customization.

Overall, the card design concept is rooted in the principles of simplicity, clarity, and visual hierarchy. It aims to enhance the user experience by presenting content in a visually pleasing and easily digestible format, enabling users to quickly and intuitively navigate through information and make informed decisions.

Closure

Closure is a fundamental concept in design and user-experience disciplines. It refers to the perception that an object or design is whole, complete, or finished, even if some parts are missing or not explicitly shown.

When users encounter a design or interface, their minds actively seek to make sense of the information presented to them. Closure allows users to mentally fill in missing parts based on their past experiences and knowledge. It enables them to understand the design and interact with it more effectively.

In design, closure can be achieved through various techniques. One common approach is the use of gestalt principles, such as proximity, similarity, and symmetry. By arranging elements in a way that suggests a relationship or pattern, designers can trigger the user's mind to complete the missing pieces.

In the field of user-experience, closure plays a crucial role in enhancing usability and reducing cognitive load. Users appreciate designs that provide closure because they require less mental effort to comprehend. When users can easily understand a design, they are more likely to feel satisfied and accomplished.

Closure is not limited to visual design; it also applies to the overall user experience. For example, in a multi-step task, providing clear indications of progress and completion can give users a sense of closure and confidence in their progress.

In conclusion, closure is a vital element in design and user-experience disciplines. It allows users to perceive designs as complete and comprehend them effortlessly. By leveraging closure, designers can create effective and enjoyable experiences for users.

Color Accent

Color Accent is a design and user-experience technique used to draw attention to a specific element or area within a digital interface by applying a contrasting color. It is widely used in web and graphic design to highlight important information, actions, or interactive elements.

This technique helps users quickly identify and understand the main focus of a page, allowing them to navigate and interact with the interface more efficiently. By using a bold or distinct color, designers can create a visual hierarchy, guiding users towards the most critical content or functionality.

Color Contrast

Color contrast refers to the degree of difference between two or more colors used in a design or user interface. It is a critical aspect of both design and user experience (UX) disciplines as it plays a significant role in ensuring visual clarity, accessibility, and readability of content.

Designers use color contrast to create visual hierarchy, highlight important elements, and improve overall aesthetics. It helps guide users' attention by making important information stand out. In addition, it aids in organizing and structuring content effectively, making it easier for users to scan and comprehend.

In the context of UX, color contrast is particularly crucial for ensuring accessibility for all users, including those with visual impairments or color blindness. It allows for better legibility of text and content, making it easier for users to read and understand. A sufficient contrast ratio between text and background is necessary to meet accessibility standards and guidelines, such as the Web Content Accessibility Guidelines (WCAG).

Furthermore, color contrast also affects the overall usability and readability of digital interfaces. Insufficient contrast can lead to eye strain, discomfort, and even difficulties in distinguishing between different interface elements or content. It may create a poor user experience, causing frustration and potentially leading to users abandoning the platform or website.

Ultimately, color contrast is a fundamental aspect of design and UX that influences both the visual appeal and usability of digital products. It requires careful consideration and implementation to ensure optimal accessibility, readability, and user engagement.

Color Depth

Color depth, also known as bit depth or pixel depth, refers to the number of bits used to represent the color of a single pixel in a digital image or display. In the context of design and user experience disciplines, color depth plays a crucial role in determining the visual quality and fidelity of digital graphics, photos, and videos.

The higher the color depth, the more colors can be represented, resulting in richer and more detailed images. Color depth is measured in bits per pixel (bpp) and typically ranges from 1 bpp (black and white) to 32 bpp (true color). Each additional bit doubles the number of colors that can be displayed or stored.

For designers and user experience professionals, understanding and managing color depth is essential for creating visually appealing and engaging digital experiences. Careful consideration of color depth helps ensure that images and graphics retain their intended colors and visual details across different devices and platforms.

Choosing an appropriate color depth requires a balance between visual quality and file size. A higher color depth enhances the fidelity of complex graphics and photographs but may increase file size and load times. On the other hand, lower color depths can result in reduced visual quality and color accuracy.

Designers must also be aware of color depth limitations in different devices and platforms, as lower color depth displays may not accurately render high-resolution images or graphics. By optimizing color depth based on the target device and media, designers can achieve the best possible visual experience for their users.

Color Distribution

Color distribution refers to the arrangement and proportion of different colors within a design or user experience. It plays a crucial role in creating visual harmony, guiding the user's attention, and evoking desired emotions. In design, color distribution is carefully planned and executed to ensure a balanced and pleasing visual composition. It involves selecting colors that complement each other and arranging them in a way that achieves a desired visual hierarchy and emphasis.

Proper color distribution helps in establishing a cohesive and unified design by creating a sense of order and structure. In the context of user experience, color distribution is essential for guiding users' attention and providing clarity. It helps in highlighting important elements, such as call-to-action buttons or important information, and creating a visual flow that leads users through the interface in a logical and intuitive manner.

By using contrasting colors, designers can ensure that key elements stand out and are easily noticeable to users. Thinking about color distribution is crucial for designing accessible experiences. By considering factors like color blindness and contrast sensitivity, designers can ensure that their designs are inclusive and readable for all users. Proper color distribution can help in conveying information effectively, reducing cognitive load, and improving the overall usability of the interface. In conclusion, color distribution is a fundamental aspect of design and user experience, influencing the aesthetic appeal, coherence, and functionality of a design. By strategically arranging and proportioning colors, designers can create visually pleasing, accessible, and user-friendly experiences.

Color Dominance

Color Dominance refers to the principle of design in which one color is more prominent or visually dominant than others in a composition or user interface. It is a fundamental concept in both Design and User-Experience (UX) disciplines, as color plays a crucial role in conveying information, influencing emotions, and guiding user attention.

In design, color dominance can be achieved through various techniques, such as using a large area or element in a dominant color, using high-contrast colors, or simply placing a strategically positioned element in a dominant color. By establishing color dominance, designers can create focal points, draw attention to important information or elements, and create a visually cohesive and harmonious composition.

In UX, color dominance is especially important for guiding users and communicating hierarchy. By assigning a dominant color to primary actions or important elements, designers can make them stand out and ensure that users easily recognize and interact with them. Conversely, less important or secondary elements can be presented in less dominant colors or even grayscale to reduce visual clutter and prevent distractions.

When implementing color dominance, designers must consider factors such as contrast, accessibility, and cultural associations. The dominant color should provide sufficient contrast against the background or other colors to ensure legibility and visibility. It is also important to choose colors that are accessible to individuals with color vision deficiencies.

Additionally, cultural associations and personal experiences can influence the perceived dominance of certain colors, so designers should be mindful of the intended audience and context. Overall, color dominance is a powerful tool for designers and UX practitioners to create visual impact, guide user attention, and communicate effectively. Understanding and applying this principle can enhance the visual appeal, usability, and overall user experience of a design or interface.

Color Harmony

Color harmony is a fundamental principle in the fields of design and user experience. It refers to the aesthetically pleasing arrangement of colors in a design or interface that creates a sense of balance, unity, and visual appeal.

In design, color harmony is achieved by selecting and combining colors in a way that complements and enhances each other. The goal is to create a harmonious color scheme that evokes the desired emotions, communicates the intended message, and engages the audience. This involves considering factors such as color psychology, cultural associations, and color theory principles.

In user experience, color harmony plays a crucial role in creating a visually cohesive and user-friendly interface. Consistent use of harmonious colors helps users navigate and understand the interface efficiently. It aids in establishing visual hierarchy, highlighting important elements, and guiding users towards desired actions.

Color harmony can be achieved through various color schemes, including complementary, analogous, triadic, and monochromatic. Complementary colors, for example, are opposite on the color wheel and create strong contrast and vibrancy when used together. Analogous colors, on the other hand, are adjacent to each other and create a sense of harmony and flow. Triadic colors form a triangle on the color wheel and provide a balanced combination. Monochromatic colors restrict the use of a single hue in different shades, tints, and tones.

Ultimately, color harmony is an essential aspect of design and user experience as it significantly impacts the overall visual appeal, usability, and effectiveness of a design or interface. By carefully considering and implementing color harmony principles, designers and user experience professionals aim to create engaging and memorable experiences for their audiences.

Color Hierarchy

A color hierarchy refers to the arrangement and organization of colors in a design or user experience (UX) to create visual hierarchy, convey information, and guide user attention. It involves the use of a primary color, secondary colors, and accent colors to establish a visual structure and emphasize different elements within a design.

In the context of design, establishing a color hierarchy helps users understand the importance and relationships between various information and design elements. The primary color is typically used for the most important elements such as headings or key buttons, while secondary colors are used for less important but still meaningful elements, such as subheadings or secondary buttons. Accent colors are used sparingly to draw attention to specific details or interactive elements, like links or call-to-action buttons.

By utilizing a color hierarchy, designers ensure that content is easily scannable and understood by users, as the differences in color aid in visually organizing the information. For example, a darker, bolder primary color might indicate more critical information, while a lighter secondary color might indicate less important details. This way, users can quickly navigate the design and find what they are looking for without being overwhelmed. In the user-experience discipline, color hierarchy plays a crucial role in helping users understand the structure of a website or application.

It guides users through different sections and highlights interactive elements, thereby enhancing the overall usability and accessibility of the platform. The appropriate use of color hierarchy also improves visual aesthetics, making the design more visually appealing and engaging for users.

Overall, a well-implemented color hierarchy is essential for effective communication and usability in design and user experience. By using strategic color choices, designers and UX professionals can create visually pleasing and user-friendly experiences that guide users through content and interactions.

Color Monotony

Color monotony, in the context of design and user experience disciplines, refers to the excessive use of the same or similar colors throughout a design or user interface. It occurs when there is a lack of variation and contrast in the color scheme, resulting in a visually uninteresting or monotonous experience for the user.

Color is a powerful tool in design, as it can evoke emotions, convey meaning, and guide the user's attention. However, when a design relies too heavily on a single color or a limited color palette, it can create a sense of sameness and make it difficult for users to distinguish different elements or sections within the interface.

Color monotony can have a negative impact on user experience by causing cognitive overload and reducing visual interest. When users are presented with a monotonous color scheme, they may struggle to navigate and process information effectively. It can also lead to a lack of visual hierarchy, making it challenging for users to prioritize or understand the importance of certain elements.

Designers and user experience professionals should aim to create visually engaging and aesthetically pleasing experiences by employing a well-balanced and varied color palette. By using contrasting colors, gradients, or subtle variations within a color family, designers can add depth, hierarchy, and visual interest to their designs.

Color Psychology

Color psychology is the study of how different colors can affect human emotions and behaviors in the context of design and user experience disciplines. It seeks to understand the psychological response that people have to the use of specific colors in various design elements, such as websites, apps, logos, and advertisements.

Colors have the power to evoke certain emotions and associations in people, and understanding this can be crucial in creating effective and impactful designs. For example, warm colors like red, orange, and yellow are often associated with feelings of energy, passion, and excitement, while cool colors like blue and green can evoke a sense of calmness, relaxation, and trust.

Additionally, cultural and personal experiences can also influence how individuals perceive and respond to colors. For instance, certain colors may have different connotations in different cultures, and personal preferences or associations can shape one's emotional response to a particular color.

In the field of user experience, color psychology plays a key role in guiding designers in their color choices to create positive user interactions and experiences. By understanding how color can impact emotions, designers can strategically use colors to convey desired messages, create visual hierarchy, and establish a cohesive brand identity. For example, using contrasting colors can help draw attention to important elements on a webpage, while harmonious color schemes can create a sense of balance and coherence.

Overall, color psychology offers valuable insights into how colors can influence human psychology and behavior, allowing designers to create visually appealing and user-friendly designs that evoke the desired emotions and facilitate positive user experiences.

Color Saturation

Color saturation refers to the intensity or purity of a color. It represents the amount of gray in a color, with highly saturated colors appearing vivid and vibrant, and desaturated colors appearing more muted and dull.

In the context of design and user experience disciplines, color saturation plays a significant role in conveying meaning, attracting attention, and enhancing visual aesthetics. By adjusting the saturation of colors, designers can create a variety of effects and elicit different emotional responses from users.

Color Temperature

Answer

Color temperature refers to the measure of the warmth or coolness of a light source, such as a screen or a physical light bulb. This concept is particularly relevant in the fields of design and user experience as it greatly impacts the way individuals perceive and interact with visual content.

Color temperature is measured in Kelvin (K), where lower temperatures indicate warmer or reddish light, and higher temperatures indicate cooler or bluish light. For instance, a candle flame has a low color temperature of around 1800K, while a bright sunny day has a high color temperature of approximately 5000K-6500K.

In the context of design and user experience, color temperature is a crucial consideration when creating interfaces, graphics, or visual elements. The choice of color temperature greatly affects the mood, readability, and overall user engagement. Warmer color temperatures tend to evoke a sense of coziness, intimacy, and relaxation. They are often used in contexts where comfort and familiarity are desired, such as in personal blogs or entertainment websites.

On the other hand, cooler color temperatures convey a sense of professionalism, efficiency, and focus. They are commonly used in business and corporate-oriented interfaces, where clarity and productivity are key aspects. This cool lighting is often seen in office spaces or e-commerce platforms.

By understanding and utilizing color temperature appropriately, designers can effectively communicate their intended messages, influence emotional responses, and enhance the overall user experience.

Color Value

A color value, in the context of design and user-experience disciplines, refers to the specific code or representation assigned to a color in a digital or visual medium. It is a numerical or symbolic value that allows designers and developers to precisely define and communicate colors to ensure consistency and accuracy in their work.

In design and user-experience disciplines, color values are typically expressed using various color models such as RGB (Red, Green, Blue), CMYK (Cyan, Magenta, Yellow, Black), HSL (Hue, Saturation, Lightness), and Hexadecimal. These models provide different ways to quantify and represent colors, allowing designers to achieve their desired visual outcomes and understand the behavior of colors in different mediums.

Each color model has its own system of assigning values to colors. For example, in RGB, each color channel (Red, Green, Blue) is assigned a value ranging from 0 to 255, where 0 represents no presence of the color and 255 represents the maximum intensity of that color. These values can be combined to create millions of different colors.

Color values play a crucial role in creating aesthetically pleasing designs and intuitive user experiences. They help designers establish visual hierarchies, evoke specific emotions, ensure accessibility, and maintain brand consistency. By defining color values, designers and developers can easily communicate color specifications to colleagues, clients, or printers, fostering efficient collaboration and accurate color reproduction.

Color Vibrancy

Color Vibrancy refers to the intensity and liveliness of colors used in a design or user experience. It is an important element in both disciplines as it can greatly impact the overall aesthetic appeal and emotional response of a design.

In design, color vibrancy plays a crucial role in attracting and capturing the attention of users. Vibrant colors have a powerful visual impact and can create a sense of excitement and engagement. They can also evoke specific emotions or moods, influencing the overall perception of a design. For example, warm and bright colors like red and orange can convey a sense of energy and urgency, while cool colors like blue and green can evoke a calming and serene atmosphere.

In user experience, color vibrancy can enhance the usability and readability of a design. Colors with high vibrancy can differentiate important elements, such as buttons or links, from the rest of the content, guiding users' attention and improving usability. Additionally, vibrant colors can improve the legibility of text, making it easier for users to read and comprehend the information.

However, it is essential to use color vibrancy judiciously, as an excessive use of vibrant colors can lead to visual overload and fatigue. Finding the right balance between vibrancy and subtlety is crucial to avoid overwhelming users and ensure a pleasant and enjoyable user experience. By carefully selecting and applying vibrant colors, designers and user experience professionals can create visually appealing and engaging designs that effectively communicate the desired message and achieve the intended goals.

Complementary Colors

Complementary colors, in the context of design and user experience disciplines, refer to a color scheme that consists of two colors that are opposite each other on the color wheel. These colors create a strong contrast and tend to enhance each other when paired together. The concept of complementary colors is based on the theory that colors with opposite properties create visual interest and harmony when used together.

When applied to design, complementary colors are often used to create vibrant and eye-catching visuals. By leveraging the stark contrast between the two colors, designers can bring attention to specific elements, draw focus, and enhance the overall visual impact of a composition. Complementary color schemes are commonly used in marketing materials, advertisements, website designs, and user interfaces to make key elements stand out and create a memorable visual experience for users.

Consistency in Color

Consistency in color refers to the deliberate use of a consistent color scheme across design elements and user interfaces in order to create a visually harmonious and cohesive experience for users. It is an essential principle in both the design and user-experience disciplines, as it helps create familiarity and ease of use, resulting in a more intuitive and enjoyable interaction for users.

In design, consistency in color ensures that elements such as buttons, links, headings, and backgrounds share a common palette, creating a visual hierarchy and aiding in the recognition and understanding of different components. By consistently using a specific range of colors, designers can establish a coherent and recognizable visual identity for their brand or product, which helps users navigate and interact with the interface more efficiently.

In user experience, consistency in color plays a crucial role in guiding users' attention and signaling interactivity. By associating specific colors with particular actions or states, such as highlighting active links or indicating errors with red text, users can quickly understand the meaning and purpose behind different elements, reducing cognitive load and increasing efficiency. Consistency in color also enhances visual feedback, providing users with clear indications of their current position in a process or the success of their actions.

Overall, consistency in color is a fundamental principle in design and user experience that ensures a cohesive and visually pleasing experience for users. It promotes brand recognition, facilitates navigation, and improves the overall usability and user satisfaction of a product or interface.

Consistency in Elements

Consistency in design and user-experience disciplines refers to the practice of maintaining uniformity and coherence in the elements and interactions of a design system or user interface. It ensures that design components, such as colors, typography, icons, and layout, are presented consistently across different screens and contexts, providing a seamless and intuitive experience for users.

Consistency plays a crucial role in enhancing usability and learnability by reducing cognitive load and improving user engagement. When users encounter consistent design patterns and interactions throughout a website or application, they can easily transfer their knowledge from one part of the interface to another, allowing for a more intuitive navigation and understanding of the system.

Consistency in Style

Consistency in style refers to the use of a uniform and cohesive visual language throughout a design or user experience. It involves maintaining a consistent aesthetic in terms of colors, typography, layout, and other visual elements. Consistency in style helps to establish a sense of familiarity and coherence, aiding users in navigating and understanding digital interfaces.

Within the context of design and user experience disciplines, consistency in style plays a crucial role in creating user-friendly and visually appealing products. It ensures that different elements within a design, such as buttons, menus, or icons, have a consistent look and feel, allowing users to easily recognize and interact with them. By adhering to a consistent style, designers can enhance usability, reduce cognitive load, and foster a positive user experience.

Continuation

Design is the process of creating a visually appealing and functional solution for a given problem. It involves the strategic and intentional arrangement of elements such as color, typography, imagery, and layout to communicate a particular message or facilitate a specific action. Design disciplines aim to address the needs of users, while also considering aesthetic and technical aspects.

User-Experience (UX) refers to the overall experience and satisfaction that a person has when interacting with a product, system, or service. It encompasses various aspects such as usability, usefulness, accessibility, and visual appeal. UX disciplines focus on understanding users' needs, behaviors, and preferences to design intuitive and enjoyable experiences that meet their expectations.

Contrast in Scale

Contrast in Scale refers to the variation in size between different elements or components within a design or user experience. It is a design principle that can be applied to create visual interest, hierarchy, and emphasis. In the context of design and user experience disciplines, Contrast in Scale is commonly used to guide the viewer's attention and create a sense of hierarchy.

By employing different sizes for various elements, designers can strategically direct the user's focus to the most important or relevant parts of a design or interface. When applied effectively, Contrast in Scale can help establish a visual hierarchy, ensuring that important information stands out and captures the user's attention. For example, headlines or titles may be designed larger than supporting text to differentiate their importance.

Similarly, navigation elements such as buttons or links may be made larger to make them more prominent and easily clickable. Another application of Contrast in Scale is to create visual interest by juxtaposing elements of different sizes.

This contrast can add dynamism and elegance to a design, making it visually appealing and engaging. For instance, mixing large images or visual elements with smaller text or icons can create a sense of balance and proportion. In summary, Contrast in Scale is a design principle that involves varying the size of elements within a design or user experience. It is used to direct the viewer's attention, establish visual hierarchy, and create visual interest. By employing different sizes for various elements, designers can effectively guide the user's focus and enhance the overall user experience.

Contrast in Shape

The concept of contrast in shape is a fundamental principle in both design and user-experience disciplines. It refers to the deliberate use of different shapes within a composition to create visual interest, hierarchy, and emphasis. By juxtaposing contrasting shapes, designers can create a dynamic and engaging visual experience for users.

In design, contrast in shape can be achieved by using various geometric forms, such as circles, squares, triangles, or irregular shapes. By combining and arranging these shapes in different sizes, orientations, and positions, designers can create a strong visual contrast that captures the viewer's attention. This contrast can be further enhanced by using contrasting colors, textures, or patterns within the shapes.

In user-experience design, contrast in shape plays a crucial role in guiding users' attention and providing them with visual cues. By using distinct shapes for different elements, such as buttons or links, designers can easily differentiate interactive elements from non-interactive ones. This helps users quickly understand where they can interact with an interface, enhancing the overall usability and intuitiveness of a design.

Moreover, contrast in shape can also be used to establish a sense of hierarchy and organization within a layout. By using different shapes for headings, subheadings, and body text, designers can create a visually appealing structure that guides users through the content. This makes it easier for users to scan and understand information, improving the overall user experience.

Contrast in Texture

Contrast in texture refers to the variation in the tactile qualities or surface characteristics of different elements within a design or user experience. It involves the deliberate use of different textures to create visual interest, enhance usability, and evoke specific emotions or associations.

In the context of design, contrast in texture can be achieved through various techniques, such as using different materials, patterns, or finishes. For example, a website may incorporate a combination of smooth surfaces, rough textures, and glossy or matte finishes to create a visually dynamic and engaging user interface. In the realm of user experience, contrast in texture is important for enhancing usability and guiding user interactions.

By employing distinct textures, designers can differentiate between interactive elements and non-interactive ones, providing users with clear cues about what they can engage with. For instance, a textured button or icon can be easily distinguishable from surrounding elements, making it more intuitive for users to identify and click on.

Contrasting textures can also contribute to the overall aesthetic appeal of a design or experience, evoking specific feelings or associations. A soft, plush texture may create a sense of comfort or luxury, while a rough, gritty texture can convey a more rugged or industrial aesthetic. By strategically incorporating different textures, designers can elicit desired emotional responses from users, helping to convey a brand's personality or establish a desired atmosphere.

In conclusion, contrast in texture is a fundamental principle in design and user experience that involves the deliberate variation in tactile qualities or surface characteristics. It not only enhances visual interest but also improves usability and evokes specific emotions or associations. By leveraging different textures, designers can create engaging and intuitive experiences that effectively communicate their intended message or brand personality.

Contrast

Contrast refers to the difference between elements in a design or user experience, specifically in terms of their visual characteristics such as color, size, shape, texture, or value. It is a fundamental principle used to create emphasis, hierarchy, and visual interest in a composition.

By contrasting elements, designers can highlight important information, guide users' attention, and create a sense of order and structure. Contrast can be achieved through various techniques, such as using contrasting colors (e.g., dark vs. light), different font sizes or weights, contrasting shapes (e.g., round vs. square), or varying the spacing between elements.

Convergence

Convergence in the design and user-experience disciplines refers to the integration and harmonization of various elements and aspects within a product or service. It signifies the seamless blending of multiple components, such as technology, functionality, aesthetics, and usability, to create a cohesive and holistic user experience.

Design convergence involves the alignment of visual elements, typography, color schemes, and layout to ensure consistency and coherency across different screens, platforms, and devices. It aims to provide a unified and recognizable brand identity, enabling users to easily navigate and interact with the product or service regardless of the context or medium they are using.

Depth Illusion

Depth illusion, in the context of Design and User-Experience (UX) disciplines, refers to the technique or effect used to create the perception of depth in a two-dimensional (2D) space. It provides visual cues that trick the viewer's mind into perceiving objects as having depth and dimension, even though they are displayed on a flat surface.

By strategically incorporating various visual elements such as shading, texture, perspective, and overlapping, designers aim to create a sense of depth and three-dimensionality in their digital or physical designs. Depth illusion is particularly crucial in UX design, as it enhances the user's understanding of hierarchies, relationships between elements, and the spatial layout of a product or interface.

Depth Perception

Depth Perception refers to the ability of a user to accurately perceive the distance and spatial relationships between objects in a three-dimensional space. In the context of design and user-experience disciplines, depth perception helps users understand the layout and hierarchy of content, providing visual cues that assist in navigating and interacting with the user interface.

Designers use various techniques to create depth perception in digital interfaces, such as using shadows, gradients, and perspective. These visual cues help users differentiate between foreground and background elements, determine the relative sizes and positions of objects, and perceive the depth of layered content.

Depth Simulation

Depth simulation is a design and user-experience technique that aims to create an illusion of depth on a two-dimensional screen or surface. It is used to enhance the visual experience and engagement of the user by adding a sense of spatial relationships between elements, similar to how objects appear in the real world with varying distances.

Through the use of techniques such as shading, shadowing, perspective, and layering, depth simulation provides visual cues that help users perceive the position and hierarchy of elements on a screen. This allows for more intuitive navigation and interaction, as well as a more immersive and realistic experience.

Depth of Field

Depth of Field is a visual design principle used in the field of User Experience (UX) and Design. It refers to the perceived distance between objects in a visual composition or layout. By strategically manipulating the depth of field, designers can guide users' attention and create a visually engaging and intuitive user experience.

Depth of Field is achieved by controlling the focus, sharpness, and blurriness of different elements within a composition. The foreground, midground, and background elements are arranged in a way that creates a sense of depth, making the composition appear more immersive and three-dimensional.

A shallow depth of field is often used to emphasize a specific element or focal point, while blurring out the surrounding elements. This technique helps direct users' attention to the most important or relevant content on the screen, allowing them to quickly and easily understand the hierarchy of information.

On the other hand, a deep depth of field is useful for presenting a detailed and comprehensive view of a scene. This approach is commonly used in data visualizations or complex interfaces where all elements need to be equally recognizable and accessible.

Depth of Field plays a crucial role in enhancing the user's experience by creating a visually pleasing and organized layout. By carefully considering the placement and clarity of elements, designers can guide users' focus, improve readability, and make interfaces more intuitive to navigate.

Directional Cues

Directional cues in the context of design and user-experience disciplines refer to visual elements or design techniques that guide and direct the user's attention towards specific areas or actions within a digital interface.

These cues are strategically placed to help users navigate, understand, and interact with the interface in a more intuitive and efficient manner. By leveraging human psychology and visual perception, directional cues serve as visual signposts that communicate important information or indicate desired actions.

Divergence

Divergence refers to a critical process in the disciplines of Design and User-Experience (UX) where ideas, concepts, or design alternatives are explored and expanded upon in order to generate a wide range of possibilities. It involves pushing the boundaries, diverging from traditional or obvious solutions, and exploring multiple directions to foster innovative and creative outcomes.

This iterative process of divergence encourages designers and UX practitioners to think beyond the obvious, challenge assumptions, and explore various perspectives to find unique and inventive solutions. It involves generating a rich multitude of ideas, options, and variations, often through brainstorming, ideation sessions, or other creative techniques.

Dominance

Dominance in the context of Design and User-Experience disciplines refers to a principle that emphasizes the importance of creating a visual hierarchy within a design or interface. It involves highlighting the most significant elements and organizing them in a way that guides the user's attention and helps them understand the content or functionality of a system more effectively.

By establishing dominance, designers can communicate a clear message and make it easier for users to navigate through the interface. This principle involves several aspects, such as size, color, contrast, placement, and proportion. Designers emphasize important elements by making them larger, using vivid colors, and placing them strategically within the layout. They also utilize contrast to create visual separation between different elements and guide the user's eyes to the most important ones.

Duotone

Duotone is a design technique commonly used in user-experience disciplines that involves the process of converting an image into two colors. It provides a visually appealing and modern aesthetic to the design.

The technique involves choosing two contrasting colors that are applied to different parts of the image. One color is used for the highlights or lighter areas, while the other color is used for the shadows or darker areas. These colors can be selected based on the brand's color scheme or the desired visual impact.

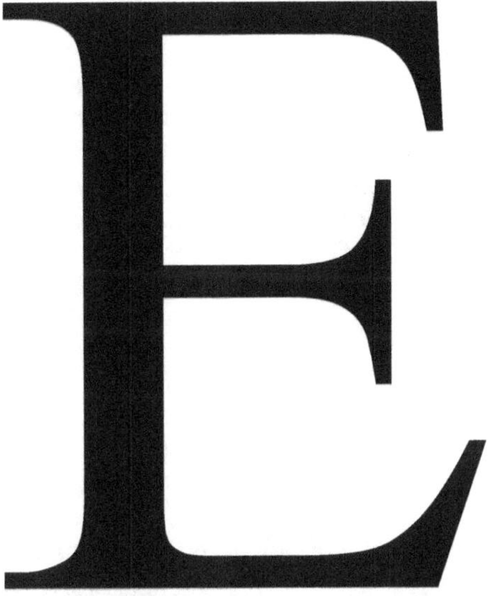

Emphasis Through Color

Emphasis through color is a design technique used in the disciplines of design and user experience to draw attention to certain elements or to create a focal point within a visual composition.

Color, as a visual element, has the power to evoke emotions, communicate meanings, and create hierarchy. In the context of design and user experience, emphasis through color refers to the intentional use of color to make certain elements stand out and capture the viewer's attention. It is achieved by using contrasting colors, vibrant hues, or by simply using a color that is different from the surrounding elements.

Emphasis Through Contrast

Emphasis through contrast is a design principle used in the disciplines of design and user experience to draw attention to a specific element or section of a visual composition or interface by highlighting it through deliberate differences in various design properties.

By creating contrasting elements, such as differences in size, color, shape, texture, or position, emphasis through contrast helps guide users' attention and communicate hierarchy within a design. This technique is commonly employed to draw users' focus towards important information, interactive elements, or call-to-action buttons, optimizing usability and user engagement.

Emphasis Through Position

Emphasis Through Position is a principle used in design and user-experience disciplines that involves using spatial placement to draw attention to certain elements and content. This technique relies on the fact that human eye naturally follows a certain reading pattern and places more importance on elements that are positioned in prominent areas.

By strategically positioning key elements or content, designers can guide users' attention and encourage specific actions or interactions. For example, in a website layout, placing the primary call-to-action button in a more prominent position, such as at the top of the page or the center, can increase the chances of users noticing and clicking on it.

Emphasis Through Size

Emphasis through size is a design principle used in both the fields of design and user experience to draw attention to specific elements or information by altering their size. It involves selectively enlarging or decreasing the size of certain elements, such as text, graphics, or buttons, to create visual hierarchy and guide users' attention.

In design, emphasis through size plays a crucial role in creating a focal point within a layout. By increasing the size of a particular element, such as a headline or a call-to-action button, designers can make it more visually prominent and instantly catch the viewers' attention. This technique helps communicate the importance of specific content or actions, while also establishing a visual hierarchy that guides users through the design.

In the realm of user experience, emphasis through size is employed to highlight key information or interactive elements to improve usability and aid in task completion. By enlarging critical elements, such as primary navigation links or form fields, users can quickly identify their intended actions and reduce cognitive load. This design approach helps users understand the content structure, quickly find what they need, and efficiently interact with the interface.

When effectively used, emphasis through size enhances the overall visual appeal, ensures important information isn't overlooked, and provides a seamless user experience. However, it is important to maintain balance and consistency while using this principle, as excessive size variation may lead to a cluttered or unbalanced design. Additionally, considering accessibility guidelines is essential to ensure that users with visual impairments can also perceive the emphasized elements through alternative means like assistive technologies.

Emphasis

Emphasis, in the context of design and user-experience disciplines, refers to the technique used to bring attention to certain elements or content within a design or user interface. It involves creating visual hierarchy and guiding the user's attention to important or relevant information. Emphasis is crucial for effective communication and engagement, as it helps users quickly understand and navigate through a design or interface.

Designers use various methods to create emphasis, such as size, color, contrast, and placement. By using size, designers can make certain elements larger and stand out from the rest of the content, drawing attention to important information. Color can also be used to create emphasis by using a bold or contrasting color for specific elements. Contrast, specifically in terms of brightness or saturation, can be employed to make elements stand out from their surroundings. Placement, on the other hand, involves strategically positioning elements in a design to guide the user's attention and create emphasis.

Fibonacci Sequence

The Fibonacci Sequence is a mathematical sequence that follows a specific pattern, where each number is the sum of the two preceding ones.

In the context of Design and User Experience disciplines, the Fibonacci Sequence can be utilized to create aesthetically pleasing and visually balanced designs. This concept is known as the "Golden Ratio," which is derived from the Fibonacci Sequence.

Figure-Ground Relationship

The figure-ground relationship refers to the perceptual organization of a design or user experience where a clear distinction is made between the subject of focus (figure) and the surrounding elements (ground). This relationship helps create hierarchy, balance, and clarity within the design or user experience.

In design, the figure is the main element or focal point that stands out and captures the viewer's attention. It is the element that designers want to emphasize or draw attention to. The ground, on the other hand, refers to the background or the elements that serve as a backdrop for the figure. The ground is usually less prominent and is used to support the figure, providing context and enhancing its visibility.

By establishing a clear figure-ground relationship, designers can effectively communicate the intended message or purpose of a design. The figure can be emphasized through various design techniques such as size, color contrast, position, or visual hierarchy. This helps guide the viewer's attention and creates a sense of order and organization within the composition.

In user experience design, the figure-ground relationship plays a crucial role in enhancing usability and user comprehension. By distinguishing the figure from the ground, users can easily identify interactive elements, such as buttons or links, and understand the hierarchy of information presented on a screen. This allows for effortless navigation, improved user flow, and more intuitive interactions.

Flat Design

Flat design is a minimalist design approach that focuses on simplicity and two-dimensional flat shapes, with a strong emphasis on clean lines and minimal use of gradients, textures, and realistic effects. This design style originated from Microsoft's Windows 8 operating system, aiming to create a visually appealing and user-friendly interface. Flat design removes unnecessary details, reducing visual clutter and enhancing usability.

In flat design, elements are presented in a straightforward and intuitive manner, making it easy for users to understand and interact with the interface. Flat design utilizes bold and vibrant colors, which help to draw attention to important elements and create a visually engaging experience. The lack of complex visual effects ensures that the interface remains fast and responsive, enhancing the overall user experience.

Fluid Design

Fluid design is a design approach that aims to create flexible and adaptable user interfaces by allowing elements to resize and rearrange themselves according to the screen size and resolution. It is a key principle in responsive web design and user experience (UX) design disciplines.

In fluid design, the layout and elements of a website or application are not fixed or rigidly defined, but instead adjust to fit various devices and screen sizes seamlessly. This ensures that the content remains readable and usable regardless of whether it is viewed on a large desktop monitor or a small smartphone screen.

Focal Point Contrast

Focal Point Contrast refers to the deliberate use of contrasting elements within a design or user experience to draw attention to a specific area or element, known as the focal point. This technique is employed in the disciplines of design and user experience to guide users' attention and enhance the visual hierarchy of a design.

By utilizing elements such as color, shape, size, texture, or position, designers create contrast between the focal point and other elements in the design. This contrast helps to establish visual dominance and attract users' attention to the most important information or actions.

Focal Point Isolation

Focal Point Isolation, in the context of Design and User-Experience disciplines, refers to the technique of creating a clear and distinct visual focus on a specific element or area within a design. By isolating the focal point, designers aim to direct the user's attention to a specific element that is crucial for understanding, navigation, or interaction with the design.

This technique can be achieved by utilizing various design principles and elements such as color, contrast, size, position, and typography. Through the strategic use of these elements, designers can create a visual hierarchy that guides the user's eye towards the focal point.

Focal Point

A focal point is a specific element or area within a design or user experience that is intentionally highlighted or emphasized to attract and direct the user's attention. It is a visual anchor that helps guide users through the content or interface, making it easier for them to understand and interact with the design.

In design, the focal point is created using various techniques such as size, color, contrast, positioning, and typography. By making the focal point stand out from the surrounding elements, designers can effectively draw attention to important information or actions, encouraging users to engage with the design in a meaningful way.

Font Alignment

Font alignment refers to the positioning of text within a design or user interface, with the goal of creating visual balance and readability. It is an essential consideration in both design and user-experience disciplines, as it directly impacts the legibility and overall aesthetics of the content.

In design, font alignment involves aligning the text in a way that complements the overall composition. There are three primary alignment options: left-aligned, right-aligned, and center-aligned. Left alignment is commonly used in most cases, as it provides a more natural reading flow for users who are accustomed to reading from left to right. Right alignment can be used sparingly for visual variety or to create emphasis. Center alignment is often used for headings or titles, creating a visually balanced appearance.

In the context of user experience, font alignment plays a critical role in enhancing readability and usability. Proper alignment ensures that the text is easy to read and follow, allowing users to effortlessly navigate and comprehend the content. It also contributes to a sense of hierarchy, where headings and subheadings are aligned differently to distinguish their importance and guide users through the information.

By considering font alignment in design and user experience, designers and developers can create visually appealing and functional interfaces that effectively communicate the desired message. Whether it's a website, app, or print material, font alignment is a fundamental element that ensures the content is accessible and engaging to the target audience.

Font Contrast

Font contrast refers to the degree of difference between two or more fonts used in a design or user experience. It refers to the variation in font styles, weights, sizes, or colors that are applied to the textual elements within a design or interface. The purpose of font contrast is to create visual hierarchy, enhance readability, and guide users' attention to important information.

In design, font contrast can be achieved by using different font families with distinctive characteristics, such as serif and sans-serif fonts. By combining fonts with different styles and weights, designers can create a visual contrast that helps users differentiate between headings, subheadings, and body text. For example, using a bold and large font for headings, while using a lighter and smaller font for body text, creates a clear contrast that makes the content easier to scan and read.

In user experience, font contrast plays a crucial role in improving the usability and accessibility of digital interfaces. By utilizing proper font contrast, designers can ensure that text is easily readable for users with different visual abilities. Poor font contrast can lead to legibility issues, particularly for users with low vision or color blindness. Therefore, it is important to carefully select font combinations that provide enough contrast between foreground and background elements.

Overall, font contrast is an essential aspect of design and user experience as it contributes to both the aesthetic appeal and functional effectiveness of a design or interface. By using varying font styles, weights, sizes, or colors, designers can create a visually pleasing and accessible experience that effectively communicates information to users.

Font Pairing

Font pairing refers to the strategic combination of two or more fonts in design and user-experience disciplines. It involves choosing fonts that complement and enhance each other when used together to create visual harmony and legibility.

The primary purpose of font pairing is to establish a coherent and well-balanced typographic hierarchy that aids in effective communication and improves user experience. By carefully selecting fonts that contrast in style, weight, or mood, designers can create a visual hierarchy that guides the reader's eye and emphasizes important elements within a design.

When selecting fonts for pairing, typographical considerations play a vital role. Fonts should have complementary characteristics, such as similar proportions, x-height, or overall style. Combining fonts that are too similar can make it difficult for users to distinguish different levels of information, while fonts that are too contrasting can create confusion and detract from the overall design aesthetic.

Effective font pairing requires a strong understanding of typography principles, including font families, font weights, and font styles. Designers must consider readability, legibility, and the overall mood or message they want to convey. By experimenting with different font combinations and analyzing the results, designers can ensure that the chosen fonts not only enhance each other but also align with the brand's identity and target audience preferences.

Ultimately, font pairing is a nuanced art form that requires a keen eye for detail and a thorough understanding of the principles of design and user experience. It plays a crucial role in creating visually appealing, communicative, and user-friendly designs across various mediums, including websites, mobile applications, print materials, and more.

Font Weight

Font weight refers to the thickness or darkness of a font's characters. It is an important element in design and user-experience disciplines as it plays a vital role in conveying visual hierarchy and enhancing readability.

In design, font weight is used to create contrast and emphasis between different elements of a layout. By choosing appropriate font weights, designers can highlight important information or headlines, make certain text stand out, or create a sense of structure and organization. For example, a bold font weight may be used to draw attention to a call-to-action button or a subheading, while a lighter weight may be used for body text to improve legibility.

Foreshortening

Foreshortening is a visual technique used in design and user-experience disciplines to create a sense of depth and perspective within a two-dimensional medium.

It involves distorting the size and proportion of objects or elements in a composition to convey their relative distance from the viewer. By exaggerating the dimensions of objects that are closer to the viewer and compressing those that are farther away, foreshortening helps create a realistic sense of depth and spatial relationships.

Gestalt Principles

Gestalt principles are a set of principles utilized in design and user experience disciplines to understand how individuals perceive and make sense of visual stimuli. These principles were developed from Gestalt psychology, which emphasizes that the human mind organizes and interprets complex information in a holistic and unified manner, rather than as separate and individual elements.

One of the fundamental principles is the principle of proximity, which states that objects or elements that are close to each other are perceived as belonging together. This principle encourages designers to group related elements in close proximity to one another, which helps users recognize patterns, relationships, and hierarchies within a design or user interface.

Another important principle is the principle of similarity, which suggests that elements that share similar visual characteristics, such as shape, size, color, or texture, are perceived as being part of the same group. By utilizing this principle, designers can create visual hierarchies and organize information in a clear and structured manner.

Furthermore, the principle of closure asserts that humans tend to fill in missing information and perceive incomplete shapes or objects as complete. Designers can use this principle to create simple and minimalist designs that encourage users to mentally complete the missing pieces, resulting in a more engaging and interactive experience.

Overall, the application of Gestalt principles in design and user experience disciplines allows designers to create more intuitive, visually appealing, and user-friendly interfaces by leveraging the innate ways in which individuals perceive and interpret visual information.

Golden Ratio

The Golden Ratio is a design principle used in the fields of design and user experience to create aesthetically pleasing and harmonious compositions. It is a mathematical ratio defined as approximately 1.618 and is often represented by the Greek letter phi (φ).

In design, the Golden Ratio is used to establish balanced proportions by dividing a composition into two parts, where the ratio of the smaller part to the larger part is equal to the ratio of the larger part to the whole. This ratio is believed to create a sense of visual harmony and balance that is appealing to the human eye.

By incorporating the Golden Ratio, designers can create layouts and visual elements that are visually pleasing and engaging. It can be applied to various design elements such as typography, grid layouts, image placement, and object dimensions. By using these proportions, designers can guide the user's attention, create focal points, and establish a sense of order and hierarchy.

In the user experience discipline, the Golden Ratio can be applied to interface design, particularly in the placement and sizing of elements. By aligning buttons, form fields, and other interface elements using the Golden Ratio, designers can create a visually pleasing and balanced user interface that improves the overall user experience.

Golden Triangle

The Golden Triangle is a design principle commonly used in the fields of design and user experience (UX) disciplines. It refers to the triangular pattern that is formed when users visually scan a webpage or any other visual medium.

According to the Golden Triangle principle, users tend to focus their attention on the upper-left corner of a webpage, then move diagonally across to the upper right, and finally scan along the bottom left of the screen. This pattern is often associated with the letter 'F' in terms of its shape.

Gradient

A gradient refers to a visual effect in design that involves a smooth transition between two or more colors or shades. It is commonly used in both print and digital media to create depth, add visual interest, and enhance the user experience.

In the context of design, gradients are often applied to backgrounds, buttons, icons, and other visual elements to achieve a more dynamic and appealing look. They can be simple, consisting of two colors, or complex, featuring multiple hues that seamlessly blend together. Gradients can be linear, where the colors transition in a straight line, or radial, where the colors radiate outward from a center point.

Gradients are especially prominent in user experience (UX) design, as they can help convey hierarchy, indicate interactivity, and guide users' attention. By using gradients, designers can create a sense of depth and dimension, making interfaces more visually engaging and intuitive to navigate. For example, a button with a gradient background can appear more clickable and stand out from other elements on the screen.

It is worth noting that gradients should be used tastefully and strategically, taking into consideration factors such as brand identity, accessibility, and the overall design goals. Care should be taken to ensure that the contrast between the colors used in the gradient is sufficient for users with visual impairments to perceive the design properly.

Grid

A grid is a foundational design tool used in various disciplines, including Design and User Experience (UX). In the context of these fields, a grid refers to a system of horizontal and vertical lines that divide a layout into consistent and proportionate sections. This structured framework helps designers organize and align elements, enabling a harmonious and balanced composition. The purpose of using a grid in design is to establish a sense of order and structure. By defining a set of predetermined columns and rows, designers can create a visual hierarchy and ensure that elements align with precision. This helps to provide a clear and intuitive user experience, as users can easily navigate and understand the information presented. Grids also assist in establishing a consistent visual language across multiple screens or devices.

By adapting the grid to different screen sizes or breakpoints, designers can ensure that the layout remains responsive and adaptable. This is particularly important in today's digital landscape, where websites and applications need to be accessible on various devices, such as desktops, tablets, and smartphones. Moreover, grids can help designers achieve a sense of balance and rhythm in their compositions.

By organizing elements within the grid's framework, designers can create visual connections and establish a flow that guides the user's eye. This enhances the overall aesthetic appeal and improves the user's engagement with the design. In conclusion, a grid is a fundamental design tool used in Design and User Experience disciplines. It provides a structured framework for organizing and aligning elements, resulting in a visually pleasing and user-friendly composition. The use of grids helps designers establish order, consistency, and balance, ultimately enhancing the overall user experience.

Harmony

Harmony in the context of design and user-experience disciplines refers to the overall balance and unity created in a design, resulting in a visually pleasing and cohesive experience for the users. It involves the thoughtful arrangement and integration of various design elements, such as colors, typography, shapes, textures, and whitespace, to create a sense of order and unity.

Harmony is achieved when all the design elements work together harmoniously, without one element overpowering or conflicting with another. This is accomplished through careful consideration of visual hierarchy, proportion, and rhythm. Visual hierarchy establishes the importance and relationship between different elements, allowing users to easily navigate and understand the design. Proportion ensures that the size and scale of elements are harmonious and balanced, creating a sense of visual stability. Rhythm refers to the repetition and variation of design elements, creating a sense of movement and flow.

Hierarchy of Fonts

In design and user-experience disciplines, the hierarchy of fonts refers to the organization and prioritization of different fonts or typefaces within a design or layout. This hierarchy helps guide the reader's attention and establish a visual hierarchy. The use of different fonts can convey different levels of importance, emphasis, and hierarchy within a design.

For example, headings or titles may be set in a bold and larger font size to stand out and grab attention. Subheadings or section titles may use a slightly smaller and less bold font style, indicating a lower level of importance. Body text or regular content may be set in a standard font size and style, providing information and supporting the main headings.

By establishing a clear hierarchy of fonts, designers can effectively guide the reader's attention and enhance the overall user experience.

A consistent and deliberate use of fonts can help convey the intended message and create visual harmony within the design. It can also aid in the readability and comprehension of the content, making it easier for users to navigate and understand the information provided.

In conclusion, the hierarchy of fonts is an essential aspect of design and user experience. By carefully selecting and organizing different fonts, designers can establish a visual hierarchy that guides the reader's attention and enhances the overall user experience. The use of different fonts can convey different levels of importance and help create a cohesive and visually appealing design.

Hierarchy

Hierarchy, in the context of design and user experience disciplines, refers to the organization and arrangement of elements within a visual composition or user interface to convey information, guide user attention, and communicate relative importance.

In design, hierarchy is used to create visual order and structure, ensuring that users can easily understand the content and navigate through the information. It involves arranging elements such as text, images, and interactive components in a way that clearly communicates their relationships and importance. By establishing a clear hierarchy, designers can guide users' attention to the most critical information and actions, improving the overall usability and user experience.

High Key and Low Key Lighting

High Key Lighting refers to a lighting technique in design and user-experience disciplines that involves the use of bright and evenly distributed lighting across a scene or subject. This technique aims to create a sense of positivity, energy, and clarity in the visual presentation. By illuminating the entire scene or subject with strong light, high key lighting eliminates shadows and reduces contrast, resulting in a soft and well-lit environment.

On the other hand, Low Key Lighting is a lighting technique that involves the use of dim or selective lighting in design and user-experience disciplines. It aims to create a sense of mystery, drama, and intensity by emphasizing contrasts, shadows, and darkness. Low key lighting often uses spotlights or focused light sources to highlight specific areas or subjects, creating a chiaroscuro effect that adds depth and visual interest to the scene.

Isolation

Isolation is a principle in design and user experience that refers to the degree to which an element or feature of a product is visually or conceptually distinct from its surroundings. It involves creating a clear separation between different elements or groups of elements to promote clarity and enhance the user's focus. In design, isolation can be achieved through the use of white space, contrast, or visual cues such as borders or underlines. By isolating specific elements, designers can guide the user's attention and make it easier for them to understand the purpose or function of each element.

For example, isolating buttons or interactive elements can help users quickly identify where they can take action. In terms of user experience, isolation can also refer to the separation of different tasks or functionalities within a system. This can be achieved through hierarchical organization, grouping related elements together, or providing clear visual indicators. Isolation helps users understand the relationships and dependencies between different parts of a system, making it easier for them to navigate and accomplish their goals.

Overall, the principle of isolation in design and user experience aims to enhance clarity, focus, and ease of use. By visually separating and organizing elements, designers can create more intuitive and user-friendly interfaces, leading to a better overall user experience.

Isometric Design

Isometric design is a visual representation of three-dimensional objects on a two-dimensional plane, which creates a sense of depth and realism. It is a technique used in design and user experience disciplines to create visually appealing and engaging designs.

In isometric design, the objects are rendered with parallel lines that are perpendicular to the plane of the design. This technique allows for the depiction of objects from multiple angles, giving the illusion of depth and spatial relationships. The lines in the design are typically drawn at a 30-degree angle to the horizontal and vertical axes.

Isometric design is popular in various design fields, including architecture, product design, and graphic design. It is often used to showcase complex structures or concepts in a simplified and visually appealing manner. By utilizing isometric design, designers can convey information more effectively and engage users through interactive and immersive experiences.

In user experience design, isometric design is employed to create user interfaces that are visually appealing and intuitive. The three-dimensional perspective of isometric design helps users understand the spatial relationships between different elements on the screen, making it easier to navigate and interact with the interface. Isometric design can also create a sense of depth and hierarchy, making it easier for users to differentiate between different elements and understand their importance.

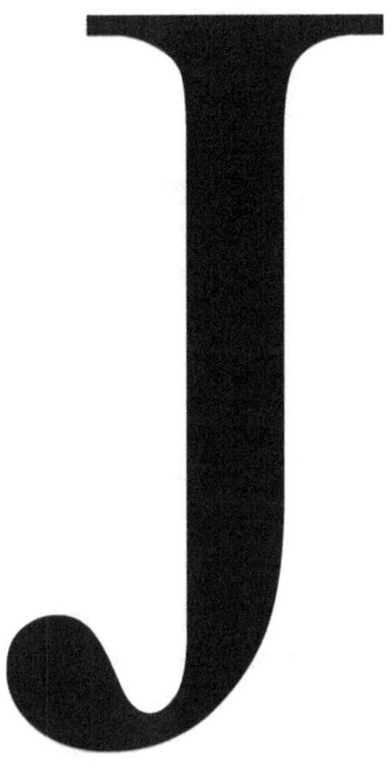

Jakob's Law

Jakob's Law, named after web usability expert Jakob Nielsen, states that users spend most of their time on other websites and online platforms, rather than on a specific one. Therefore, users expect a certain level of consistency and familiarity when interacting with websites or digital interfaces.

In the context of design and user-experience disciplines, Jakob's Law emphasizes the importance of adhering to well-established design conventions and using familiar patterns. By doing so, designers can create intuitive and user-friendly experiences that align with user expectations.

Journey mapping workshops

A journey mapping workshop is a collaborative and interactive session conducted within the context of Design and User-Experience disciplines. In this session, designers, stakeholders, and other relevant team members come together to visualize and understand the end-to-end journey of the users or customers.

The workshop typically involves various activities and discussions aimed at gaining insights into the users' experiences, emotions, and pain points at different touchpoints throughout their journey with a product or service. By mapping out the user journey, the workshop participants can identify areas of improvement, as well as opportunities to enhance the overall user experience.

Journey orchestration

Journey orchestration is a process within the design and user-experience disciplines that focuses on mapping out and coordinating the various interactions and touchpoints a user has with a product or service. It involves understanding the user's journey from the initial point of contact to the ultimate goal or outcome, and creating a seamless and engaging experience throughout.

Through the use of data and insights, journey orchestration aims to identify and address the pain points and opportunities for improvement along the user's journey. This process involves analyzing user behaviors, preferences, and needs, and designing personalized experiences that meet those requirements.

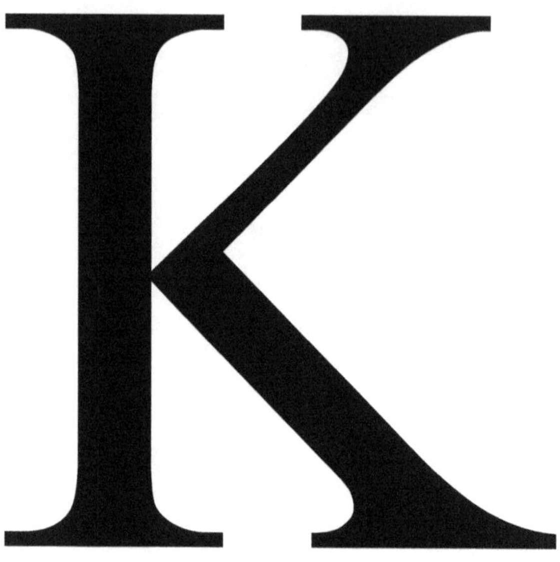

Knowledge sharing platforms

A knowledge sharing platform in the context of Design and User-Experience disciplines refers to an online platform or tool that enables the exchange and dissemination of knowledge, information, and best practices related to design and user experience. It serves as a central hub where individuals within the industry can share, collaborate, and learn from one another.

These platforms typically facilitate the sharing of various types of content, such as articles, case studies, research papers, tutorials, and videos. They provide a space for designers and user experience professionals to showcase their work, discuss their ideas, and seek feedback and critique from the community.

Knowledge transfer methods

Knowledge transfer methods in the context of Design and User-Experience disciplines refer to the strategies and techniques used to effectively share knowledge and expertise among individuals or teams within these fields.

These methods aim to facilitate the transfer of valuable insights, best practices, and design principles from experienced designers to less experienced ones, enabling a more efficient and consistent approach to the design process and the creation of user-centered experiences.

Knowledge transfer

Knowledge transfer in the context of Design and User-Experience disciplines refers to the process of sharing information, skills, and insights from one individual or group to another, with the intention of improving the overall understanding and proficiency in these fields.

It involves the dissemination of both explicit and tacit knowledge, encompassing theoretical principles, practical techniques, and problem-solving approaches. Explicit knowledge refers to information that can be easily articulated, codified, and transferred through documents, manuals, or training materials. Tacit knowledge, on the other hand, refers to the less tangible knowledge that is embedded in individuals' experiences, intuitions, and expertise, which is often difficult to communicate directly or formally.

Knowledge transfer can be achieved through various methods, such as mentorship, collaboration, workshops, research papers, conferences, and online platforms. It requires effective communication, active participation, and a supportive learning environment to bridge the knowledge gap between the knowledge provider (experts, practitioners) and the knowledge recipient (novices, learners).

By facilitating knowledge transfer, Design and User-Experience disciplines aim to enhance the development and application of design thinking, problem-solving skills, and creative solutions. It enables individuals and teams to learn from past experiences, leverage existing knowledge, and collectively contribute to the advancement of the discipline. Ultimately, knowledge transfer plays a vital role in improving the quality of design outcomes, user experiences, and fostering innovation in various industries and sectors.

Layer Hierarchy

In the context of design and user experience disciplines, layer hierarchy refers to the arrangement and organization of visual elements within a design, with the purpose of guiding user attention and creating a sense of depth and hierarchy. It involves the use of different layers, or levels, to establish a visual order and structure.

Layer hierarchy is achieved by strategically placing elements in foreground and background positions, assigning varying levels of importance and emphasis. This can be done through the use of size, color, contrast, spacing, and texture, among other visual cues.

The topmost layer typically contains the most important and prominent elements, drawing the user's attention and serving as the focal point. Subsequent layers may contain supporting elements or secondary information. The purpose of layer hierarchy is to guide the user's eye through the design, helping them quickly understand the content and navigate through it effectively.

By establishing a clear layer hierarchy, designers can create a sense of visual depth and dimension, making the design more engaging and visually appealing. This helps users distinguish between different elements and prioritize information based on its importance. A well-executed layer hierarchy enhances the overall user experience, making the design more intuitive and user-friendly.

In conclusion, layer hierarchy is a fundamental principle in design and user experience, allowing designers to create visual order, guide user attention, and enhance the overall usability of a design.

Layering

Layering refers to the technique in design and user-experience disciplines where elements are organized and arranged in a way that creates a visual hierarchy and enhances user understanding and interaction. It involves the skillful arrangement of various components to create a sense of depth and order within a design, allowing users to easily navigate and comprehend the content.

In the context of design, layering involves placing elements such as images, text, and interactive elements on different levels within a layout. This arrangement allows certain elements to appear closer or farther away, giving the design a three-dimensional feel. By manipulating the placement, size, and transparency of these elements, designers can create an illusion of depth and guide users' attention to specific focal points. This technique improves the visual flow of information and encourages users to interact with the design in a more intuitive manner.

In the realm of user experience, layering is employed to improve usability and user comprehension. Through the careful structuring of information, designers can prioritize critical content, making it more prominent and accessible to users. Layering can also be utilized to group related elements together, facilitating user understanding and reducing cognitive load. The visual cues provided by layering can help users navigate through complex interfaces and easily identify the relationships between different elements.

Overall, layering plays a crucial role in enhancing the visual and interactive aspects of design and user experience. By employing this technique, designers can create visually appealing and user-friendly interfaces that effectively communicate information and guide users' interactions.

Leading Lines

Leading lines, in the context of design and user-experience disciplines, refer to visual elements that are strategically placed within a design composition to guide the viewer's eye towards a specific focal point or to create a sense of movement and flow. These lines can be either literal lines or implied lines created through the use of various design elements.

By using leading lines effectively, designers can control the viewer's gaze and direct their attention to important information, such as call-to-action buttons or key content. This technique helps to improve the overall user experience by reducing cognitive load and making it easier for users to navigate and interact with a design.

Material Design

Material Design is a design language developed by Google that aims to create a consistent and intuitive user experience across different platforms and devices. It focuses on using grid layouts, bold colors, and meaningful animations to guide and engage users.

Material Design is characterized by its use of flat and minimalistic elements, along with a three-dimensional appearance created through the strategic use of shadows and layers. It emphasizes clean and simple interfaces that prioritize clarity and ease of use.

Minimalism

Minimalism in the context of Design and User-Experience (UX) disciplines is a philosophy that advocates for simplicity, clarity, and a focus on essential elements.

Design minimalism emphasizes the removal of unnecessary elements, reducing complexity, and distilling a design to its core elements. It aims to create clean, uncluttered visual compositions that enhance user engagement and understanding. Minimalist designs often employ generous white space, limited color palettes, and simple typography to convey a sense of elegance and sophistication. By eliminating non-essential elements, minimalist designs can help users navigate and interact with interfaces more intuitively, resulting in a more streamlined user experience.

Monochromatic Color Schemes

A monochromatic color scheme in the context of design and user-experience disciplines refers to a harmonious combination of colors that are derived from a single base hue. In this color scheme, different shades, tints, and tones of the same color are used to create a visually appealing and cohesive design.

A monochromatic color scheme offers simplicity and elegance by utilizing variations of a single color. It allows designers to create depth and interest without the complexity of using multiple colors. By working with different intensities of the base hue, designers can play with light and shadow to create a sense of balance and harmony.

Movement

Movement in the context of Design and User-Experience disciplines refers to the visual perception of motion or change within a design. It is the techniques and principles used to create the illusion of movement or guide the user's attention throughout a design.

Movement can be achieved through various design elements such as lines, shapes, colors, and typography. For example, using lines that converge towards a specific point can create the perception of movement towards that point. Similarly, contrasting colors can be used to create visual vibrations or fluctuations, adding a sense of movement to the design.

In User-Experience design, movement is crucial for guiding users and helping them understand how to interact with a product or interface. It is used to direct attention, indicate functionality or hierarchy, and provide visual feedback. For instance, subtle animations can be employed to highlight important elements or indicate changes in state, making the user experience more intuitive and engaging.

Movement can also evoke certain emotions or convey a sense of energy and dynamism. Fast or erratic movements can create a feeling of urgency or excitement, while slow and smooth movements can result in a soothing and calming effect. Understanding the impact of movement on user perceptions and emotions is essential for creating effective and meaningful designs.

Negative Space

Negative space, in the context of design and user-experience disciplines, refers to the empty or unoccupied areas in a design composition or layout. It is also known as white space or blank space. Negative space plays a crucial role in creating balance, clarity, and visual hierarchy in a design.

By intentionally leaving areas of a design empty, negative space acts as a breathing room for other design elements and content. It helps define the relationship between different elements, guiding the viewer's eye and facilitating better comprehension of the information presented.

Opacity Gradient

An opacity gradient refers to a visual effect created by gradually changing the transparency of an element or a portion of an element. In the context of design and user experience disciplines, it is often used to enhance the aesthetics and improve the readability or focus of certain elements on a webpage or interface. By applying an opacity gradient, designers can visually communicate depth, provide visual cues, or create a sense of hierarchy within the content. It allows for a smooth transition from one opacity level to another, resulting in a subtle and visually appealing effect. To create an opacity gradient, designers typically utilize CSS (Cascading Style Sheets) properties. One commonly used property is "opacity" which sets the transparency level for an element and its contents. By specifying different opacity values at various points of the element, designers can achieve the desired gradient effect. For example, consider a webpage with a background image and a text overlay. By applying an opacity gradient to the text, starting from fully transparent to partially opaque, the text gradually becomes more visible and stands out from the background. This technique can be particularly useful when dealing with images or illustrations that have contrasting colors or patterns. Overall, an opacity gradient is a valuable tool in the designer's toolbox for creating unique and visually engaging user experiences. It allows for the manipulation of transparency levels to guide the user's attention, emphasize important content, or simply add an aesthetically pleasing touch to the overall design.

Opacity

Opacity is a design and user-experience (UX) concept that refers to the level of transparency or ability to see through an element on a webpage or in an application interface. It is one of the fundamental properties used to control the visual appearance and hierarchy of UI components.

In design disciplines, opacity is typically represented by a numeric value ranging from 0 to 1, with 0 being completely transparent or invisible, and 1 being fully opaque or solid. This value determines the visual clarity and legibility of the content and elements placed behind or within the transparent object.

Overlapping Elements

Overlapping elements, in the context of design and user-experience (UX) disciplines, refers to the technique of positioning two or more elements in such a way that they partially or fully occupy the same space on a webpage or interface. This overlapping arrangement can be purposeful, serving a specific design intention or UX goal. By strategically overlapping elements, designers can create depth and dimension, add emphasis, or establish visual hierarchy within a layout. This technique allows for the blending of different design elements, such as images, text, or interactive components, resulting in visually engaging and dynamic interfaces. In terms of UX, overlapping elements can play a key role in guiding users' attention and interaction.

Through careful positioning and layering, designers can direct users' focus towards important information or interactive elements, ensuring a seamless and intuitive user experience. By incorporating overlapping elements, designers can also create visual cues or affordances, indicating to users how different elements relate to each other or how they can interact with them. It is important to note that proper implementation of overlapping elements in design and UX requires careful consideration of factors such as contrast, readability, accessibility, and overall visual coherence.

Good design practices ensure that overlapping elements do not hinder legibility or cause confusion for users. In summary, overlapping elements in design and UX involve intentionally placing two or more elements within the same space to create visual interest, enhance interactivity, guide users' attention, and establish hierarchy. Applying this technique requires thoughtful consideration and adherence to design principles to ensure a cohesive and user-friendly interface.

Overlapping elements, in the context of design and user-experience (UX) disciplines, refers to the technique of positioning two or more elements in such a way that they partially or fully occupy the same space on a webpage or interface.

By strategically overlapping elements, designers can create depth and dimension, add emphasis, or establish visual hierarchy within a layout.

Overlapping

Overlapping in the context of design and user-experience disciplines refers to the concept of elements or objects partially or entirely covering each other on a screen or page. It involves the intentional placement of design elements in a way that creates visual hierarchy, depth, and interest.

Overlapping is commonly used in user interface and web design to highlight important content, guide the user's attention, and create a sense of depth and layering. It can be achieved through various techniques such as using transparent overlays, stacking elements with different z-index values, or utilizing shadows and gradients.

Pattern Repetition

Pattern repetition is a design principle often used in the fields of Design and User-Experience (UX) to create visually unified and coherent experiences for users.

Pattern repetition involves the regular and consistent use of recurring visual elements throughout a design or user interface. These elements could include shapes, colors, textures, icons, typography, or even specific layout arrangements.The repetition of patterns in design serves several purposes. Firstly, it helps create a sense of harmony and consistency, which is essential for establishing a cohesive visual identity and branding. By repeating certain elements, a design becomes instantly recognizable and associated with a particular brand or product.

Additionally, pattern repetition can aid in guiding users' attention and navigation within a user interface. By using consistent visual cues, users can familiarize themselves with the design and quickly understand how to interact with it. This improves the overall usability of a product or website.

Furthermore, pattern repetition can also bring a sense of organization and structure to a design. By repeating certain layout arrangements or visual elements, designers can establish a clear hierarchy and grouping of content. This helps users easily identify related information and navigate through a design more intuitively.

In conclusion, pattern repetition in the context of Design and User-Experience disciplines refers to the deliberate and consistent use of recurring visual elements to create a visually unified, coherent, and user-friendly experience. It plays a crucial role in establishing brand identity, aiding navigation, and organizing content within a design.

Pattern Variation

A pattern variation refers to a modification or adaptation made to an existing design pattern in the context of design and user-experience disciplines. Design patterns are reusable solutions to commonly occurring design problems, and they provide a way to solve these problems in a structured and proven manner.

However, in specific cases, the original design pattern may need to be adjusted or customized to better suit the unique requirements of a particular design or user experience. Pattern variations can occur at different levels, such as visual design, interaction design, or information architecture. They involve altering certain aspects of the original pattern while still retaining its core principles and intentions.

These modifications aim to improve usability, enhance aesthetics, or incorporate additional functionality to meet the specific needs of the design or user experience. Pattern variations often arise from the desire to create a more tailored and personalized experience for users. By adapting an existing pattern, designers can ensure that the design solution is better aligned with the specific goals, preferences, and expectations of the target audience.

It also allows for innovation and differentiation, as designers have the flexibility to explore creative alternatives while still adhering to established design principles. In conclusion, pattern variations are modifications made to existing design patterns to better align them with the specific requirements and preferences of a particular design or user experience. This helps in creating a more customized and tailored solution that meets the unique needs of users while still leveraging the proven effectiveness of established design patterns.

Pattern

A pattern, in the context of Design and User-Experience disciplines, refers to a repeatable solution to a common problem or challenge faced in the design process. It is a proven formula or method that has been identified through research, analysis, and testing, to address a particular design problem effectively. Patterns are created and shared among designers to provide a framework for approaching and solving design problems in a consistent and efficient manner.

A design pattern typically consists of a set of guidelines, principles, or best practices that guide the decision-making process and help designers make informed choices.

It can cover various aspects of design, including layout, navigation, interaction, visual aesthetics, and information organization. By leveraging patterns, designers can draw from established solutions, instead of reinventing the wheel, speeding up the design process and ensuring a more user-friendly and intuitive final product.

Perspective

Perspective in the context of Design and User-Experience (UX) disciplines refers to the viewpoint or mental framework through which users perceive and interact with a product or service. It encompasses the user's understanding, expectations, and overall experience while engaging with a design solution.

Perspective is crucial in creating effective and engaging designs as it allows designers to empathize with users, understand their needs, and design solutions that address those needs. By considering the perspective of the user, designers can create intuitive and user-friendly experiences that align with user expectations and enhance overall satisfaction.

An effective way to gain perspective is through user research and testing. This involves observing and gathering feedback from users to understand their goals, preferences, and pain points. By gathering insights from real users, designers can uncover valuable information that helps them align their designs with user expectations and preferences.

Perspective also applies to the visual aspect of design. It involves considering the visual composition, hierarchy, and placement of elements to guide the user's attention and create a balanced and visually appealing experience. By using visual cues and proper layout, designers can direct the user's perspective towards key elements and interactions within a design.

Proportion

A proportion refers to the relationship or ratio between different elements or parts of a design or user experience. It involves the careful arrangement and scaling of various visual or interactive components in order to create a harmonious and aesthetically pleasing composition.

In the context of design, proportion plays a critical role in ensuring balance, harmony, and coherence within a layout or interface. It involves determining the ideal size, scale, and placement of different elements to create a visually appealing hierarchy and flow. Proportional relationships can be established through the use of grids, guidelines, and established design principles such as the rule of thirds or the golden ratio.

Proximity

In the design and user-experience disciplines, proximity refers to the visual and spatial relationship between elements in a design or interface. It is the principle that states that objects that are close to each other are perceived as related or grouped together.

The concept of proximity is used to create order, hierarchy, and structure in a design. By placing related elements close together, designers can communicate their relationship and help users understand the content or functionality more easily. Proximity helps reduce cognitive load by organizing information in a way that is intuitive and logical.

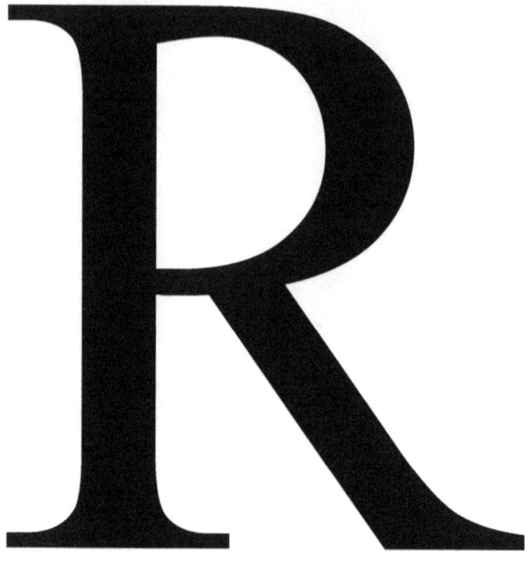

Realism

Realism, in the context of Design and User-Experience disciplines, refers to an approach that aims to create designs or experiences that closely mimic the real world. It involves designing interfaces, graphics, and interactions that mirror real-life objects, actions, and behaviors.

The principle of realism is rooted in the belief that designs that resemble familiar, real-world elements are more intuitive and easier to understand for users. By leveraging users' existing knowledge and mental models, realistic designs help reduce cognitive load, improving usability and enhancing the overall user experience.

Reflection

Reflection is a key process within the disciplines of Design and User-Experience, aiming to enhance the iterative development of products and services. It involves a systematic review and evaluation of the design process, the usability of a product or service, and the overall user experience.

Reflection in Design and User-Experience disciplines involves analyzing and critically assessing various aspects of a design project. This includes evaluating the effectiveness of design choices, understanding user needs and behaviors, and identifying areas for improvement. Through reflection, designers can gain insights into how their design decisions impact the user experience and make informed adjustments to enhance usability and overall product/service quality.

Repetition of Elements

The repetition of elements refers to the use of the same or similar design elements throughout a design or user-experience, in order to create consistency, enhance visual appeal, and improve user comprehension and usability.

In the context of design, repetition helps to establish a visual rhythm and a unified look and feel. By repeating certain elements such as colors, shapes, typography, or images, designers can create a cohesive and harmonious design that is visually pleasing and easy to navigate. Consistency in the use of these elements provides a sense of familiarity and reinforces the brand identity or overall design concept. Users can easily recognize and interpret repeated elements, which contributes to a positive user experience as they become more comfortable and proficient in using the interface.

Similarly, in the field of user experience, repetition plays a crucial role in enhancing usability and user comprehension. Consistently repeating familiar design elements such as buttons, icons, navigation menus, or interaction patterns across different pages or sections of a website or application allows users to easily understand and navigate through the interface. Repetition creates predictability and reduces cognitive load, as users can rely on their past interactions to guide their behavior and decision-making. This ultimately leads to a more efficient and satisfying user experience.

Repetition

Repetition, in the context of Design and User-Experience disciplines, refers to the intentional use of recurring elements or patterns in a design. It involves repeating specific visual elements, such as shapes, colors, fonts, or images, throughout a design or a user interface.

The use of repetition in design serves several purposes. Firstly, it helps to establish visual consistency and coherence within a design. By repeating elements, designers create a sense of rhythm and harmony, making the design more aesthetically pleasing and easier to navigate for users. Consistent repetition also helps to reinforce the brand identity and create a sense of familiarity and trust among users.

Rhythm

Rhythm refers to the regular repetition or pattern of elements in a design or user experience, creating a sense of visually pleasing movement and flow. It is one of the fundamental principles of design and plays a crucial role in creating a cohesive and harmonious composition.

In the context of design, rhythm can be achieved through various techniques, such as the repetition of shapes, colors, lines, or textures. By repeating these elements in a consistent and predictable manner, designers can establish a visual rhythm that guides the viewer's eye and creates a sense of unity and organization. Rhythm can also be created through the use of alternating or progressive patterns, where elements change gradually or in a sequence.

In the field of user experience, rhythm is essential for creating intuitive and easy-to-use interfaces. Consistency in the placement and visual appearance of interactive elements, such as buttons or navigation menus, helps users develop a mental model of the application or website, allowing them to navigate and interact with ease. Rhythmic patterns in animations and transitions can also enhance the user experience by providing visual cues and feedback.

Rule of Thirds

The Rule of Thirds is a fundamental principle in design and user-experience disciplines that guides the placement of content within a visual composition. It involves dividing the composition into a 3x3 grid, creating nine equal-sized rectangles. The four points where the lines intersect are known as the "points of interest" or "power points".

By placing key elements of the design or user interface along these lines or at the intersection points, the Rule of Thirds can help create a visually balanced and compelling composition. This technique draws the viewer's attention to these important elements and helps establish hierarchy and visual flow. It also creates a more dynamic and engaging layout, compared to a design with elements placed perfectly centered.

Scale

Scale, in the context of Design and User-Experience disciplines, refers to the size, dimensions, and proportions of elements within a design or interface.

Scale is a fundamental principle that dictates how elements are sized in relation to one another and the overall composition. It helps create hierarchy, establish visual balance, and guide users' attention to the most important elements.

When considering scale in design, it involves determining the relative size of different elements based on their importance and the desired visual impact. Larger elements often draw more attention and convey importance, while smaller elements signify lesser significance. By carefully manipulating scale, designers can communicate relationships, emphasize key content, and enhance the overall user experience.

Using scale effectively can also help establish a sense of unity and coherence in a design. By maintaining consistent proportions and sizes across various elements, designers can create a harmonious visual experience that feels cohesive and organized.

Additionally, scale can be used strategically to improve the usability of interfaces. For example, scaling up frequently used or interactive elements can make them more accessible and easier to interact with, while scaling down less important elements can reduce clutter and distractions.

In conclusion, scale plays a crucial role in designing visually appealing and user-friendly interfaces. By carefully considering the size and proportions of elements, designers can create compelling compositions that engage users and effectively communicate information.

Shadow

Shadow is a visual effect created by placing a dark or translucent replication of an object parallel to its actual form. In the context of design and user experience (UX) disciplines, shadow plays a vital role in enhancing the overall visual appeal and usability of digital interfaces.

Shadows can be used to give depth and dimension to graphical elements, helping to differentiate and separate objects on a screen. By mimicking the way light interacts with physical objects, shadows create a sense of hierarchy, layered information, and emphasize the relationships between various elements.

Similarity

Similarity in the context of design and user-experience disciplines refers to the principle of consistency and familiarity between elements, interfaces, or experiences. It is the intentional use of shared attributes, patterns, or structures to create a cohesive and intuitive user experience.

In design, similarity is crucial for establishing visual hierarchy, making information easily scannable, and guiding users through a logical flow. Consistent use of color, typography, and layout across different sections or pages of a website or application helps users to quickly understand the relationship between different elements and navigate the interface more efficiently. By implementing consistent design patterns, users can easily transfer their knowledge and experience from one part of a product to another.

Skeuomorphism

Skeuomorphism refers to a design approach in which digital interfaces or objects imitate the physical characteristics, functionalities, or behaviors of their real-world counterparts.

Derived from the Greek words "skeuos" (container or tool) and "morphe" (shape or form), skeuomorphism can be seen in various aspects of design, such as icons, buttons, textures, and visual effects.

Split-Complementary Colors

Split-complementary colors are a color scheme used in design and user experience disciplines. This scheme consists of three colors – a base color and two additional colors that are located on each side of the base color's complement. To understand this concept, it is important to define complementary colors. Complementary colors are pairs of colors that are opposite each other on the color wheel.

The split-complementary color scheme aims to create a harmonious and balanced color palette while providing more variety than a simple complementary color scheme. By using a base color and its two adjacent complementary colors, this scheme adds depth and visual interest to the design. In terms of user experience, split-complementary colors can enhance the overall usability and aesthetics of a digital product or website.

The careful selection and use of colors can help improve legibility, highlight important elements, and guide users' attention. For example, in a user interface, the base color can be used for the overall background, while the two split-complementary colors can be applied to buttons, navigation menus, or call-to-action elements to create visual contrast and hierarchy.

This not only aids in attracting users' attention but also ensures a cohesive and visually pleasing experience. It is worth noting that while split-complementary colors offer more variety than complementary colors, they can still create a strong visual impact.

Therefore, it is important to use them judiciously and consider the context and target audience when incorporating this color scheme into a design. In conclusion, split-complementary colors are a color scheme that involves a base color and two adjacent colors to its complement. This scheme is widely used in design and user experience disciplines to create harmony, visual interest, and hierarchy in digital products or websites.

Symmetry

Symmetry is a fundamental design principle in the fields of design and user-experience (UX) that refers to a sense of balance and harmony within a visual composition. It is the concept of arranging elements or components on a page in such a way that they appear visually equal, stable, and coordinated.

In design, symmetry involves creating a mirror-like balance by dividing a composition into two parts that are identical or nearly identical. It can be achieved through various techniques such as aligning objects along a central axis, using repetitive patterns, or maintaining consistent proportions.

Symmetrical designs often convey a sense of order, formality, and elegance. In the context of UX, symmetry is important for creating a visually pleasing and easily digestible user interface. It helps in organizing information, establishing hierarchy, and supporting intuitive interactions.

By applying symmetry, UX designers can enhance the user's ability to navigate through the interface, understand its structure, and locate relevant content. Symmetrical layouts can be particularly useful in situations where users need to quickly scan and understand the content, such as in e-commerce websites, dashboards, or informational sites. However, it is important to note that not all designs require strict symmetry, and asymmetrical layouts can also be effective in creating visual interest and guiding user attention.

Overall, symmetry is a key design principle that plays a vital role in creating visually appealing and user-friendly designs. Utilizing symmetry in design and UX allows for a sense of cohesion, balance, and aesthetic satisfaction, ultimately contributing to a more enjoyable and effective user experience.

Tetradic Color Schemes

Tetradic color schemes, also known as double complementary color schemes, are a type of color palette that consists of four colors. In the design and user experience disciplines, tetradic color schemes are often used to create visually appealing and balanced compositions.

These color schemes are derived from the concept of complementary colors, which are colors that are opposite to each other on the color wheel. In a tetradic color scheme, two pairs of complementary colors are selected, resulting in a total of four colors.

When using tetradic color schemes in design, it is important to consider the balance and harmony among the colors. The two pairs of complementary colors create a vibrant and dynamic visual impact, but if not carefully chosen, they can clash and create visual disharmony. Therefore, it is crucial to consider the relationships and interactions among the four colors in terms of their hue, saturation, and brightness.

By using tetradic color schemes, designers and user experience professionals can create designs that are visually stimulating and aesthetically pleasing. These color schemes provide a wide range of colors that can be used for different elements of a design, such as backgrounds, typography, icons, and illustrations. Additionally, tetradic color schemes offer flexibility and versatility, allowing designers to create different moods and ambiances by adjusting the ratios and proportions of the colors.

Texture Consistency

Texture consistency refers to the visual and tactile qualities of elements in a design or user experience that remain uniform and coherent throughout the interface.

In the context of design, texture relates to the perception of the surface quality and feel of objects. It can be actual tactile textures or simulated visual textures that are used to create a sense of depth, dimension, and realism in a design. Texture consistency plays a crucial role in ensuring a harmonious and cohesive visual experience for users.

Texture Contrast

Texture contrast refers to the intentional use of different textures or surface qualities in a design or user experience to create visual interest, enhance readability, and improve user engagement.

Within the design discipline, texture contrast involves incorporating contrasting textures, such as rough versus smooth or matte versus shiny, to create a visual hierarchy and highlight important elements. This can be achieved through a variety of design elements, including typography, imagery, icons, and background patterns. By using contrasting textures, designers can guide the user's attention, add depth and dimension to the design, and create a more immersive user experience.

In the context of user experience, texture contrast plays a crucial role in improving the usability and accessibility of digital interfaces. By using different textures, designers can differentiate between interactive elements and static content, making it easier for users to identify and interact with buttons, links, and other interactive elements. Texture contrast can also help users with visual impairments by providing tactile cues or clear visual distinctions between different elements.

Overall, texture contrast is a powerful design principle that can enhance both the aesthetic appeal and functionality of a design or user experience. By carefully selecting and combining contrasting textures, designers can create visually compelling and engaging designs while improving usability and accessibility for users.

Texture Intensity

Texture intensity refers to the perceived degree of roughness or smoothness in a visual or tactile design element. In the context of design and user-experience (UX) disciplines, texture intensity plays a significant role in shaping the overall look and feel of a design, as well as the emotional and functional responses it elicits from users.

Designers often use texture to add depth, interest, and realism to digital or physical interfaces. By manipulating the intensity of textures, they can guide users' attention, highlight important elements, or convey specific messages. For example, a high-intensity rough texture may be used to create a sense of ruggedness or toughness in a product's design, while a low-intensity smooth texture may evoke elegance or sophistication.

Texture Overlay

A texture overlay is a design element that is used in the disciplines of design and user-experience to add visual interest, depth, and dimension to a website or application. It involves overlaying a textured image or pattern on top of an existing element or background to create a visual effect.

Texture overlays can be applied to various elements such as images, backgrounds, buttons, or even the entire interface. They are often used to create a certain mood or to enhance the overall aesthetic appeal of a design. By adding texture, designers can make elements appear more tactile and interactive, which can enhance the user's experience and engagement.

Texture Subtlety

Texture subtlety refers to the degree of variation and detail present in a texture, specifically in the context of design and user experience disciplines. It is an important aspect to consider as it can significantly impact how users perceive and interact with a design or interface.

A texture with high subtlety contains intricate and nuanced details, often requiring closer inspection to fully appreciate. This can create a sense of depth and richness, providing a visually engaging experience for users. On the other hand, a texture with low subtlety has minimal variations and may appear flat or one-dimensional.

Texture Variation

Texture variation refers to the intentional use of different surface qualities or patterns in design to create visual interest and enhance the overall user experience.

Within the disciplines of design and user experience, texture variation plays a crucial role in creating depth, hierarchy, and differentiation. It involves utilizing various textures, such as smooth and rough surfaces, intricate patterns, or tactile elements, to add visual and tactile interest to a design.

Texture

Texture, in the context of design and user experience disciplines, refers to the visual or tactile quality of a surface, object, or element. It adds depth, dimension, and richness to a design, providing both visual interest and a sense of realism.

In design, texture can be created through various techniques such as patterns, gradients, shadows, and even the choice of materials or finishes. It can be smooth or rough, glossy or matte, soft or hard, and can convey different emotions or associations. Texture is often used to enhance the usability and aesthetics of a digital interface or a physical object.

Transparency

Transparency, within the context of Design and User-Experience disciplines, refers to the principle of clear and open communication between designers, users, and stakeholders throughout the design process. It involves the deliberate sharing of information, decisions, and intentions to create a sense of trust, accountability, and understanding.

Design transparency entails being honest and open about design choices, methodologies, and objectives. Designers need to clearly communicate their intentions, design rationale, and decision-making processes to clients, users, and other relevant parties. This transparency allows stakeholders to have a comprehensive understanding of the design process, promoting informed decision-making and collaborative input.

Triadic Color Schemes

A triadic color scheme is a color scheme that uses three colors that are evenly spaced around the color wheel. In design and user-experience disciplines, triadic color schemes are often used to create a vibrant and balanced visual aesthetic.

In a triadic color scheme, the three chosen colors should have equal distance from each other on the color wheel, forming an equilateral triangle. This creates a sense of harmony and balance in the design, as the colors complement each other while still providing enough contrast.

When implementing a triadic color scheme in design, it is important to consider the dominance and balance of the colors. One color can be chosen as the dominant color, while the other two colors are used as accents. By adjusting the proportions and combinations of these colors, designers can create different visual effects and moods.

Triadic color schemes are particularly suitable for designs that aim to be eye-catching and lively, as the contrasting colors create a sense of energy and vibrancy. However, it is also important to use these color schemes with caution, as too much saturation or contrast can make the design overwhelming or chaotic.

Type Alignment

Type alignment refers to the arrangement and positioning of text elements in a design or layout. It is a fundamental aspect of visual design and typography, allowing for effective communication and visual hierarchy. In visual design, type alignment is used to create structure and organization within a design. It helps to establish a consistent and cohesive look by aligning text elements along a common axis or grid. Different types of alignments include left alignment, right alignment, center alignment, and justified alignment.

Left alignment is commonly used in Western cultures as it provides a clear and familiar reading pattern. Right alignment can be used for emphasis or to create a sense of asymmetry. Center alignment is often used for titles or headings, creating a balanced and visually pleasing effect. Justified alignment aligns text along both the left and right margins, creating a clean edge on both sides. In typography, type alignment is crucial for readability and legibility.

Proper alignment ensures that text is easy to read and understand. It also helps to establish a clear hierarchy of information, with headings and subheadings aligned differently from body text. Consistent alignment throughout a design provides a sense of order and professionalism. Overall, type alignment plays a critical role in visual design and typography, helping to create structure, hierarchy, and readability in a design or layout.

Type Anatomy

Anatomy in the context of Visual Design and Typography disciplines refers to the structure and form of letters, characters, and glyphs. It involves studying and understanding the individual components and features that make up a typeface or letterform. In typography, anatomy encompasses various elements such as the baseline, x-height, ascender, descender, stem, serif, counter, aperture, terminal, and more.

These components contribute to the overall appearance and legibility of a typeface. For example, the baseline is the imaginary line upon which characters rest, while the ascender is the part of a lowercase letter that extends above the x-height.

Understanding the anatomy of type is crucial in visual design as it allows designers to make informed decisions regarding font selection, spacing, hierarchy, and overall composition. By analyzing the individual parts of a typeface, designers can ensure that their designs are visually appealing, legible, and effectively communicate the intended message. Typography plays a significant role in various design disciplines such as graphic design, web design, and branding.

Choosing the right typeface and understanding its anatomy allows designers to create visually engaging and cohesive designs that resonate with the target audience. In conclusion, the study of anatomy in Visual Design and Typography disciplines involves analyzing the structure and form of letters, characters, and glyphs to inform design decisions. Understanding the anatomy of typefaces is instrumental in creating visually appealing and legible designs.

Type Contrast

Contrast is a fundamental principle in visual design and typography that involves creating a noticeable difference between elements in order to create visual interest and enhance clarity.

It refers to the juxtaposition of different elements, such as colors, shapes, sizes, textures, and positions, to create a distinct separation and emphasize their differences. In visual design, contrast can be achieved through various techniques. One of the most common is through the use of contrasting colors.

For example, placing a dark color against a light color or using complementary colors can create a strong visual impact and make elements stand out. Similarly, contrasting shapes and sizes can create a sense of balance and dynamism. In typography, contrast is essential for legibility and hierarchy. Differentiating between different levels of information is crucial to guide the viewer's attention and aid in comprehension. This can be accomplished by using varying font weights, sizes, and styles.
For instance, headings are often set in bold or larger fonts to distinguish them from body text. Moreover, contrast can also be achieved by using different typefaces with distinct characteristics, such as pairing a serif and a sans-serif font.

Overall, contrast plays a vital role in visual design and typography, as it helps to create visual impact, enhance readability, and establish a clear hierarchy of information. By deliberately juxtaposing different elements, designers can effectively communicate their messages and engage viewers in a visually compelling manner.

Type Grid

A grid is a framework of horizontal and vertical lines used to create an organized structure within a design or layout. In the context of visual design and typography disciplines, grids serve as a guide for arranging and aligning elements harmoniously, bringing order and consistency to the overall composition.

Grids function as an underlying structure that helps designers establish a balanced and intuitive visual hierarchy. By dividing the space into columns and rows, grids provide a framework to position and align text, images, and other design elements with precision. This systematic approach ensures that each element relates cohesively to others, promoting readability, hierarchy, and visual clarity.

Type Legibility

Legibility is a fundamental concept in visual design and typography disciplines. It refers to the quality of a text's readability and clarity, particularly in terms of its visual appearance and ease of comprehension. A typographic element's legibility relies on various factors, including the choice of fonts, spacing, size, and overall layout.

The legibility of a text directly impacts its effectiveness in conveying information and facilitating communication. When text is legible, it can be easily and quickly understood by the intended audience, enhancing the overall user experience. Legible typography ensures that readers can effortlessly identify individual characters, words, and even entire sentences without experiencing any confusion or strain.

Type Readability

Type readability refers to the ease with which a typeface or a specific text can be read and understood by the intended audience. It is an important aspect in the fields of visual design and typography as it directly affects the effectiveness of communication.

In visual design, type readability involves selecting and arranging typefaces in a way that ensures clear and legible text. This includes considering factors like font size, line spacing, and contrast between the text and background. A readable typeface is one that allows the reader to easily distinguish between individual letters and words, making the text effortless to read.

Typography discipline, on the other hand, focuses on the artistic and technical aspects of letterforms, and type readability is a crucial element within it. By choosing appropriate typefaces and adjusting their characteristics, such as letter spacing and kerning, typographers can enhance the overall readability of a text. A typeface with good readability not only aids in comprehension but also conveys the intended mood and tone.

Type readability plays a significant role in effective communication as it ensures that the intended message is conveyed accurately and efficiently to the audience. Whether it is a printed document, a website, or any other visual medium, readable typefaces and well-arranged text contribute to a positive user experience. Overall, in the disciplines of visual design and typography, type readability refers to the clarity and legibility of text, achieved through the careful selection and arrangement of typefaces. It is an essential consideration in creating visually appealing and communicative designs.

Type Scale

Scale refers to the size, proportion, and relationship of elements within a design. In visual design and typography, scale helps create hierarchy, establish visual weight, and enhance readability.

When designing a layout or composition, the use of different scales allows for a more engaging and dynamic design. It enables the designer to guide the viewer's attention and create a visual hierarchy that emphasizes certain elements over others.

Typeface Accessibility

Typeface accessibility refers to the consideration and design of typefaces in a way that ensures readability and usability for individuals with visual impairments or other disabilities. It encompasses the concept of creating typefaces that are legible and clear, making it easier for people with diverse abilities to read and understand the content.

In the disciplines of visual design and typography, typeface accessibility involves various elements such as font size, line spacing, letterforms, stroke width, and color contrast. These factors play a crucial role in ensuring that text is easy to read and navigate, allowing individuals with disabilities to access information effectively.

Designers need to carefully select typefaces that are clear, distinguishable, and easy on the eyes, considering factors like readability and readability at different sizes and distances.

Typeface Adaptability

Typeface adaptability refers to the ability of a typeface or font to be used in various design contexts without losing its legibility, readability, or overall aesthetic appeal. It is a crucial consideration in visual design and typography disciplines as it directly impacts the effectiveness and coherence of the visual communication being created. In visual design, typeface adaptability involves selecting and utilizing typefaces that can be applied across different mediums, such as print, web, mobile, and signage, while maintaining their visual integrity and clarity.

A highly adaptable typeface can effectively communicate the intended message, evoke the desired emotions, and enhance the overall visual design regardless of the medium or platform. In typography, typeface adaptability encompasses the ability of a typeface to perform well in various typographic elements, such as headings, body text, captions, pull quotes, and other typographic treatments. An adaptable typeface should have a wide range of weights, styles, and variants, allowing designers to effectively utilize it in different typographic hierarchies and layouts.

Additionally, it should possess distinctive features, legible letterforms, appropriate proportions, and appropriate kerning and spacing to ensure optimal readability in different sizes and contexts. The adaptability of a typeface is often influenced by its design characteristics, such as x-height, stroke contrast, serifs or lack thereof, and overall style. Sans-serif typefaces are typically known for their high adaptability due to their clean, modern aesthetic and legibility across different mediums and sizes.

However, serif typefaces can also be adaptable depending on their design and intended usage. Effective typeface adaptability requires careful consideration of the design requirements, objectives, and target audience. Designers must assess whether a typeface can perform consistently across various design contexts and effectively communicate the desired message while maintaining readability and aesthetic appeal.

Overall, typeface adaptability is a fundamental aspect of visual design and typography disciplines, playing a significant role in the creation of successful and visually cohesive designs. By selecting and utilizing adaptable typefaces, designers ensure that their designs can effectively communicate and engage with the intended audience across different mediums, sizes, and typographic treatments.

Typeface Adaptation

Typeface adaptation refers to the process of modifying or customizing a typeface to suit specific design requirements or aesthetic preferences. It involves making alterations to the original typeface design, such as adjusting the proportions, changing the stroke weight, or modifying certain letterforms.

In the context of visual design and typography disciplines, typeface adaptation plays a crucial role in creating unique and visually appealing typography. Designers often need to tailor typefaces to fit within a specific design system or to convey a specific tone or style. The adaptation process can help to ensure that the typeface aligns with the overall design vision and effectively communicates the intended message.

Typeface App Design

Typeface App Design is the process of creating an application that focuses on the selection, visualization, and management of typefaces in the context of visual design and typography disciplines. This app allows users, such as designers or typographers, to explore and utilize a wide range of typefaces to enhance the visual appeal and readability of their design projects. The primary function of a Typeface App Design is to provide users with a user-friendly interface that enables them to browse, compare, and select typefaces based on their specific design needs.

The app typically offers a vast library of fonts, categorized by various criteria such as style, serif or sans-serif, and language support. Users can search for typefaces by specific keywords or filter results based on these criteria to find the most suitable fonts for their projects. In addition to font browsing, a Typeface App Design often includes features that allow users to customize and preview typefaces in real-time.

These features typically enable users to adjust font size, spacing, alignment, and other typographic settings, providing them with a comprehensive understanding of how a particular typeface will look within their design composition.

Furthermore, a Typeface App Design may also offer additional information and resources related to typography, including typeface history, usage guidelines, and best practices. This ensures that users have access to a wealth of knowledge and guidance to make informed decisions and create visually pleasing and legible designs. Overall, Typeface App Design plays a crucial role in enabling designers and typographers to enhance their creative projects by providing them with a versatile and comprehensive tool for typeface exploration, selection, and customization.

Typeface Balance

Typeface balance refers to the distribution of visual weight within a typeface design. It is a crucial aspect of visual design and typography disciplines as it determines the overall harmony, legibility, and aesthetic appeal of the text. In typography, each typeface has its own unique personality and characteristics. Some typefaces may have heavy strokes, while others have lighter strokes. Typeface balance takes into account these variations and focuses on achieving an equilibrium between the different elements of a typeface.

The balance of a typeface is typically evaluated based on its proportions, stroke thickness, and overall design. A well-balanced typeface has an even distribution of weight throughout its characters, creating a sense of harmonious visual rhythm. This ensures that the text is visually pleasing and easy to read. In visual design, typeface balance plays a crucial role in creating a composition that is visually appealing and coherent.

A balanced typeface adds structure and organization to a design, guiding the viewer's eye and creating a sense of visual hierarchy. It helps establish a clear visual message and enhances the overall aesthetic quality of the design. Achieving a balanced typeface requires careful consideration of various elements, such as contrast, proportions, and white space.

By adjusting these factors, designers can create a typeface that is visually balanced and enhances the overall design. In summary, typeface balance is the distribution of visual weight within a typeface design. It is a critical aspect of visual design and typography disciplines, ensuring that the text is legible, visually pleasing, and harmonious. By achieving a balanced typeface, designers can create compositions that are visually appealing and effectively communicate their message.

Typeface Branding

Typeface branding refers to the practice of selecting and utilizing a specific typeface or font for the purpose of representing and enhancing a brand's identity. In visual design and typography disciplines, typeface branding plays a crucial role in establishing a brand's visual identity and creating a consistent and cohesive brand experience across various mediums and touchpoints.

When it comes to typeface branding, designers carefully choose a typeface that aligns with the brand's characteristics, values, and target audience. The selected typeface should effectively communicate the brand's personality and differentiate it from competitors. Different typefaces have unique traits, such as serif or sans-serif, bold or light weights, and varying degrees of legibility. Designers consider these traits to ensure they complement the brand's messaging and evoke the desired emotions.

Typeface Clarity

Typeface clarity refers to the legibility and readability of a typeface or font. In the context of visual design and typography disciplines, it is important to ensure that the chosen typeface is clear and easy to read, especially when used in various sizes and on different mediums.

When a typeface is clear, it means that each character is distinct and easily distinguishable from one another. This helps to prevent any confusion or misinterpretation of the text. Clarity is achieved through the design of the typeface itself, such as the shape and form of the letters, as well as the spacing between them.

Readability, on the other hand, refers to how easily the text can be read and understood. It encompasses factors such as the size of the typeface, the contrast between the text and the background, and the overall design of the layout. A typeface that is highly readable ensures that readers can comfortably process the text without any strain or difficulty. To enhance typeface clarity and readability, it is important to consider the purpose and audience of the design.

Different typefaces have varying levels of clarity and readability, so it is crucial to select the most appropriate one for the intended use. Additionally, adjusting the size, leading, and kerning of the type can also contribute to better clarity and readability. Overall, typeface clarity plays a crucial role in visual design and typography. It ensures that the text is easily readable and understood by the audience, enhancing the overall effectiveness of the design.

Typeface Classification

Typeface classification is the categorization of typefaces based on their distinctive characteristics, design attributes, and historical context. It is an essential component of visual design and typography disciplines in order to understand and utilize type effectively in various design applications.

In visual design, typeface classification plays a crucial role in creating hierarchy, conveying messages, and evoking emotions. By classifying typefaces, designers can select appropriate fonts that align with the intended visual language and aesthetic of a project. Additionally, understanding the characteristics of different typefaces can assist in creating cohesive and visually appealing compositions.

In typography, a comprehensive classification system provides a structured framework for organizing typefaces into distinct categories. This classification system enables typographers to analyze and discuss typefaces in a standardized manner, allowing for more effective communication and collaboration within the field.

Typically, typefaces are classified based on various characteristics, including the overall design style, stroke contrast, letterform structure, and historical development. Some commonly recognized typeface classifications include serif, sans serif, script, blackletter, display, and monospaced.

Overall, typeface classification is an integral aspect of visual design and typography disciplines. It helps designers and typographers make informed decisions in selecting and implementing typefaces, contributing to the overall effectiveness and cohesiveness of design projects and typographic compositions.

Typeface Communication

Typeface communication refers to the use of different typefaces or fonts in visual design and typography disciplines to convey specific messages or create specific visual effects. It involves the deliberate selection and combination of typefaces to enhance the overall meaning, tone, and aesthetic of a design or typographic composition.

When used effectively, typefaces can communicate various emotions, attitudes, and characteristics. For example, serif typefaces with their decorative strokes and flourishes often evoke a sense of tradition, formality, or elegance, making them suitable for use in formal documents or prestigious branding.

On the other hand, sans-serif typefaces with their clean, modern appearance are often perceived as more casual, approachable, or contemporary, making them suitable for use in digital interfaces or informal communications.

Typeface Consistency

Typeface consistency refers to the practice of maintaining uniformity in the choice and usage of typefaces throughout a visual design or typographic project. It involves using the same typefaces or a set of complementary typefaces consistently across different contexts, elements, and sections of the design.

Consistency in typefaces helps to establish a cohesive and harmonious visual experience, allowing the viewers to easily recognize and understand the information presented. It can enhance readability, hierarchy, and overall aesthetic appeal. By adhering to a consistent typeface palette, designers can create a sense of unity, professionalism, and brand identity.

Typeface Contrast

Typeface contrast refers to the distinction between different typographic elements in a design, particularly in terms of their weight (thickness) and style. It plays a crucial role in visual design and typography disciplines as it helps create hierarchy, visual interest, and readability in a composition.

Contrast can be achieved through variations in typeface weight, such as using a bold font for headings and a lighter font for body text. This creates a clear differentiation between different levels of information and guides the reader's attention. Additionally, contrast can also be achieved by combining different typeface styles, such as pairing a serif font with a sans-serif font or contrasting a traditional typeface with a more modern one.

Typeface Design

Typeface design is a discipline within visual design and typography that involves the creation and development of fonts or typefaces. It is the process of designing the visual appearance of letters, numbers, and other characters that make up a typeface. This includes the design of the individual letterforms, as well as the overall structure and style of the typeface. In typeface design, various factors are taken into consideration, such as legibility, readability, and aesthetics.

The designer must consider how the letters and characters will look both individually and when combined into words and sentences. They also need to consider the intended use of the typeface, whether it is for print or digital media, as this can influence the design choices. The design process often begins with sketching and experimenting with different letterforms and styles. This includes exploring different stroke weights, serifs or sans serifs, and other design elements.

The designer may also make adjustments to ensure consistent spacing and proportions throughout the typeface. Typeface design requires a deep understanding of typography principles, such as kerning, tracking, and leading. It also requires knowledge of historical typefaces and lettering styles, as well as an awareness of current trends and contemporary design practices.

Overall, typeface design plays a crucial role in visual design and typography, as it is fundamental to the communication of written language. A well-designed typeface can enhance the readability and impact of a message, while a poorly-designed typeface can hinder communication and be visually unappealing.

Typeface Distinction

When it comes to visual design and typography disciplines, typeface distinction refers to the differences and variations in the design of typefaces or fonts. It relates to the unique characteristics that make each typeface distinct from the others.

Typeface distinction is crucial in visual design as it helps create hierarchy, visual interest, and readability in written communication. By choosing typefaces with contrasting characteristics, designers can effectively differentiate between headings, subheadings, body text, and other elements. This differentiation can be achieved through variations in weight, size, style, posture, and other design attributes.

Typeface Distinctiveness

Typeface distinctiveness refers to the characteristic features of a typeface that make it visually unique and distinguishable from other typefaces. It is a key consideration in the fields of visual design and typography, as it plays a crucial role in conveying meaning, enhancing readability, and creating a distinctive brand identity.

In visual design, typeface distinctiveness is important for creating a visually appealing composition. Different typefaces have their own unique personalities, which can evoke specific emotions or convey a particular style. For example, a bold and geometric typeface may be used to convey a modern and minimalistic aesthetic, while a cursive and ornate typeface may evoke a sense of elegance and sophistication. By selecting typefaces with distinct characteristics, designers can effectively communicate the intended message and establish a cohesive visual identity for their designs.

Typeface Editorial

Typeface is a fundamental element in visual design and typography disciplines. It refers to the overall design and style of a set of characters, including letters, numbers, and punctuation marks, that make up a specific font. It plays a crucial role in communication and aesthetics, influencing the overall tone and message of a design or text.

When designing a visual composition, selecting the right typeface is essential. Each typeface has its unique characteristics, such as its size, weight, and style, which can convey different emotions, moods, and meanings. Typeface choices can evoke feelings of elegance, professionalism, playfulness, or simplicity, depending on the intended message. Additionally, the legibility and readability of a typeface are crucial factors to consider to ensure optimal comprehension.

Incorporating typefaces effectively requires a deep understanding of typography principles. Designers must consider the context, purpose, and target audience of the design to make informed decisions. They should also pay attention to typographic hierarchy, ensuring that headings, subheadings, and body copy are easily distinguishable and visually balanced.

Furthermore, typeface selection should be harmonious with other design elements like color, layout, and imagery. It should create a cohesive visual language that enhances the overall user experience.

Typeface Elegance

In the context of visual design and typography disciplines, the term "typeface elegance" refers to the aesthetic quality of a typeface that exudes sophistication, refinement, and grace. It encompasses the overall visual appearance and style of the typeface, including its shape, proportions, stroke contrast, and ornamentation.

The elegance of a typeface is often achieved through the harmonious combination of various design elements. For example, a typeface with delicate serifs, slender letterforms, and subtle details can be perceived as elegant. On the other hand, a typeface with bold, robust letterforms and sharp angular edges might convey a more assertive or powerful aesthetic.

Elegance in typeface design can also be influenced by cultural and historical factors. Certain typefaces, such as the classic serif typefaces like Bodoni or Baskerville, are often associated with elegance due to their long-standing use in traditional and prestigious contexts. Conversely, contemporary typefaces that draw inspiration from modernist or minimalist design principles may convey a more modern and sleek elegance.

In the realm of visual design and typography, typeface elegance is highly valued as it can significantly impact the overall tone and perception of a design. Whether used in print or digital media, an elegantly designed typeface can uplift the visual sophistication of a composition, enhance readability, and evoke a sense of luxury or professionalism.

Typeface Emotion

Typeface Emotion in the context of Visual Design and Typography disciplines refers to the perception of emotional characteristics or associations conveyed by a particular typeface. It is the ability of a typeface to elicit specific emotional responses or create certain moods or atmospheres in a visual design or typographic composition.

Designers carefully choose typefaces based on their emotional qualities to enhance the overall impact and communication of their designs. The emotional qualities of a typeface can be influenced by various factors, including its letterforms, stroke contrast, proportions, weight, and spacing.

Typeface Expression

Typeface Expression refers to the way a typeface is designed and used to convey a specific mood, emotion, or message in visual design and typography. It involves exploring the various characteristics of a typeface, such as the weight, width, style, and overall form, to create a cohesive and impactful visual experience.

Through careful selection and manipulation of typefaces, designers can evoke different emotions and communicate different messages to their audience. For example, a typeface with bold and heavy strokes may express strength and power, while a delicate and elegant typeface may evoke a sense of sophistication and grace. Typeface Expression can also be influenced by other factors such as color, layout, and composition, to further enhance the intended message.

Typeface Family

A typeface family is a collection of related fonts that share similar design characteristics. It consists of a variety of fonts within the same style, allowing for a cohesive and consistent visual identity. In the context of visual design and typography disciplines, a typeface family is essential for creating meaningful and aesthetically pleasing communication.

By having a range of fonts within a typeface family, designers can effectively convey hierarchy and structure within a composition. Different weights, such as light, regular, and bold, provide options to emphasize or de-emphasize certain elements. Variations in italic and oblique styles allow for added expression and emphasis. Additionally, typeface families often include multiple widths, allowing for more flexibility in different layouts and formats.

Typeface Flow

Typeface Flow refers to the visual movement and arrangement of typefaces within a design composition. It encompasses the spacing, alignment, and overall harmony between different typefaces used in a layout.

The flow of typefaces plays a crucial role in enhancing readability, establishing hierarchy, and conveying the intended message of a design. In visual design and typography disciplines, typeface flow is carefully considered to create a balanced and cohesive aesthetic. It involves selecting complementary typefaces that harmonize with each other in terms of style, weight, and proportion.

The flow also includes the arrangement of type, such as the spacing between letters, words, and lines, as well as the alignment and justification of text. A well-executed typeface flow enhances the overall legibility and readability of a design. It guides the reader's eye through the content, creating a smooth and effortless reading experience.

By establishing a clear hierarchy and structure, the flow allows important information to stand out and be easily understood. When designing with type, it is important to consider the context and purpose of the project. Different typeface flows may be appropriate for different mediums, such as print or digital. Additionally, the target audience and message being communicated should also be taken into account. In summary, typeface flow is the art of strategically arranging and harmonizing typefaces within a design composition. It is a crucial aspect of visual design and typography that contributes to readability, hierarchy, and overall aesthetic appeal.

Typeface Harmony

Typeface harmony refers to the visual balance and coherence achieved through the combination and arrangement of different typefaces in visual design and typography. It involves the deliberate selection and arrangement of typefaces to create a cohesive and aesthetically pleasing design.

When multiple typefaces are used in a design, they should complement each other and create a harmonious relationship. This harmony can be achieved through various factors such as similar letterforms, x-heights, stroke weights, and styles. The combination of typefaces should be visually balanced and not compete for attention.

Typeface Identity

A typeface identity refers to the unique visual characteristics and design elements of a specific typeface. It encompasses the overall look and feel of the typeface, including its letterforms, spacing, proportions, and stylistic markings. Typeface identity plays a crucial role in visual design and typography disciplines as it helps establish a distinct and recognizable branding or visual tone for a particular text or project.

The typeface identity is determined by various factors, such as historical influences, design principles, cultural associations, and intended use. Each typeface has its own personality and conveys a specific mood or message to the audience. For example, a serif typeface may communicate a more traditional and formal tone, while a sans-serif typeface often appears modern and clean. The typeface identity can also be influenced by the designer's intentions and the context in which it is used.

Typeface Impact

The typeface Impact is a font that is commonly used in visual design and typography disciplines. It is classified as a sans-serif typeface, which means it lacks the small decorative strokes at the end of each letter.

Impact was designed by Geoffrey Lee and released in 1965 by the British type foundry Stephenson Blake. It gained popularity due to its bold and heavy appearance, making it suitable for headlines and titles that require a strong visual impact.

Its design features include wide letterforms, thick strokes, and condensed spacing between characters. These characteristics contribute to its imposing and attention-grabbing nature. The font's large x-height, which refers to the height of lowercase letters, further enhances its legibility and visibility from a distance.

Impact is commonly used for display purposes, highlighting important information or creating emphasis. It is often seen in posters, billboards, logos, and other graphic design applications where a strong visual presence is desired. Due to its bold nature, it is best suited for short sections of text rather than long blocks of continuous text.

In recent years, Impact has also gained popularity in digital mediums, particularly in meme culture, where its use has become synonymous with impactful and bold statements. It has been widely adopted online for its ability to catch attention and create an immediate visual impact within a small space.

In conclusion, Impact is a bold and attention-grabbing typeface commonly used for headlines, titles, and display purposes in visual design and typography disciplines. Its imposing design and strong visual impact make it an excellent choice for creating emphasis and catching attention in various mediums.

Typeface Innovation

Typeface innovation refers to the creation and development of new typefaces or the modification and improvement of existing typefaces in the context of visual design and typography disciplines. It involves the exploration of new forms, styles, and structures of letterforms, as well as the consideration of various factors such as legibility, readability, and aesthetics.

Innovation in typeface design is driven by the need to adapt to changing design trends, technological advancements, and cultural shifts. It allows designers to express unique personalities and convey specific messages through the use of customized typefaces.

Typeface Legibility

Typeface legibility refers to the ease with which individual letters and characters can be distinguished and recognized within a given typeface. In the context of visual design and typography disciplines, legibility plays a crucial role in effectively communicating information. Legibility is influenced by various factors, including letterform design, spacing, line length, and the overall readability of a typeface.

The primary goal of legibility is to minimize any ambiguity or confusion that may arise when reading a particular typeface. A legible typeface enables readers to effortlessly decipher and comprehend the text, enhancing the overall user experience. Typefaces with high legibility typically feature clear and distinct letterforms that allow for easy recognition of individual characters. The design of each letterform should exhibit sufficient contrast and differentiation to prevent any visual confusion.

Additionally, adequate spacing between letters and lines helps prevent characters from blending together, ensuring optimal legibility. In contrast, typefaces with low legibility can hinder the reading process, leading to reduced comprehension and potential user frustration. Poorly designed letterforms, cramped spacing, or excessive decorative elements can all contribute to decreased legibility. When selecting a typeface for a particular design project, legibility should be a primary consideration. The intended audience, context, and medium should be taken into account to ensure that the chosen typeface effectively communicates the intended message. In conclusion, typeface legibility refers to the ease with which individual letters and characters can be recognized within a specific typeface. It is a crucial aspect of visual design and typography, as it directly impacts the readability and comprehension of written content.

Typeface Logo

A typeface logo refers to a specific combination and arrangement of characters that represents a brand or a company. It is created using various typefaces, which are distinct designs of letterforms within a particular set of characters. Typography, a fundamental aspect of visual design, plays a crucial role in the creation of typeface logos.

In the discipline of visual design, a typeface logo is a visual representation of a brand identity. It showcases the name or initials of a brand, often accompanied by a symbol or graphic element. The typeface used in a logo is carefully selected to convey the brand's personality, values, and style. Different typefaces evoke different emotions and associations, allowing designers to create logos that align with the brand's desired image and target audience.

Typeface Marketing

Typeface Marketing refers to the strategic use of typography to create visual identity and communicate brand messages effectively. It is a specialized branch of marketing that focuses on using typefaces in a purposeful manner to enhance the overall aesthetic appeal and brand recognition. In the field of visual design, typography plays a crucial role in conveying the intended message to the target audience.

Typeface Marketing involves selecting appropriate fonts, sizes, weights, and spacing to create visually appealing and legible designs. By choosing the right typefaces, designers can evoke specific emotions, convey brand personality, and enhance readability. Effective Typeface Marketing requires a deep understanding of the target audience and the brand's core values.

The typeface chosen should align with the brand's identity, whether it is bold and modern, elegant and sophisticated, or playful and whimsical. Consistency in typography across different marketing materials helps build brand recognition and reinforces the brand's visual identity. In addition to aesthetics, readability is a key aspect of Typeface Marketing. The selected typefaces should be easily legible across various mediums, such as print, web, and mobile devices. Proper kerning, leading, and spacing ensure that text is clear and readable, enhancing user experience and driving engagement.

Typeface Marketing also involves creating a cohesive visual language by using typography consistently across different marketing collaterals such as advertisements, websites, and packaging. This consistency helps establish a strong brand presence and recognition. In summary, Typeface Marketing is the strategic use of typography to create an effective visual identity and communicate brand messages. It involves the careful selection of fonts, sizes, and spacing to create visually appealing and legible designs that align with the brand's values and appeal to the target audience.

Typeface Modernity

Typeface Modernity refers to a design approach that emerged during the late 18th century and early 19th century, marking a departure from the traditional or historic typefaces prevalent at the time. It represents a shift towards more simplified and geometric forms, with a focus on clean lines, minimalistic details, and rational construction.

Typeface Modernity is characterized by its neutral, objective, and functional aesthetic, aiming to achieve a sense of timelessness. This design movement was influenced by various cultural, technological, and social factors. The advent of industrialization, advancements in printing technology, and the desire for legibility and efficiency in mass communication all played roles in shaping Modern typefaces. For instance, the introduction of sans-serif typefaces, such as Futura and

Helvetica, exemplified the move towards simplicity and clarity. Modern typefaces are often associated with modernist design principles, which sought to break free from historical ornamentation and express ideas in a more direct and functional manner.

The introduction of standardized typeface classifications - such as transitional, modern, and grotesque - allowed for greater clarity and ease of use across various typographic applications. In contemporary visual design and typography, Typeface Modernity continues to be influential. Its clean, timeless aesthetic lends itself well to a wide range of applications, from websites and digital interfaces to print materials. Typeface Modernity embodies simplicity and efficiency, allowing for effective and legible communication across media.

Typeface Packaging

A typeface packaging refers to the visual design and typography discipline that involves creating the packaging for a specific typeface. Typeface packaging serves as a way to showcase and market a typeface, allowing designers and typographers to easily access and utilize the typeface in their projects.

The primary purpose of typeface packaging is to present the typeface in a visually appealing and informative manner. This includes creating a well-designed package that highlights the unique characteristics and features of the typeface, such as its style, weight, and variations. The packaging may also include additional information about the typeface, such as its origins, historical context, and recommended usage scenarios.

Typeface Pairing

Typography is a key element in visual design that focuses on the arrangement and presentation of typefaces. Typeface pairing, within the context of visual design and typography, refers to the deliberate selection and combination of two or more typefaces to create a harmonious and visually appealing design. This process involves considering various factors such as contrast, similarity, mood, and overall aesthetic goals.

The pairing of typefaces aims to create a balanced hierarchy and organize information effectively. It helps establish visual hierarchy by distinguishing different levels of content, such as headings, subheadings, and body text. By using contrasting typefaces, designers can create a clear distinction between these content levels while maintaining a cohesive and unified overall look.

Typeface Personality

Typeface Personality refers to the emotional or psychological characteristics associated with a specific typeface. In the context of Visual Design and Typography disciplines, typefaces are not just a means of communication but also a powerful tool for evoking specific emotions, setting the tone, and enhancing the overall visual experience of a design.

Each typeface has its own distinct personality and conveys different emotions or mood. For example, a typeface with clean, geometric shapes and sharp edges might evoke a sense of modernity, sophistication, and professionalism. On the other hand, a typeface with rounded forms and soft curves might convey a more friendly, approachable, and playful personality.

The personality of a typeface is often influenced by various design elements such as the proportion of strokes, x-height, serif or sans-serif classification, letter spacing, and overall style. These elements combine to create a visual language that can communicate a wide range of emotions, from elegance and authority to warmth and informality.

Understanding and choosing the appropriate typeface personality is crucial in visual design and typography as it helps designers effectively convey the desired message, establish the right atmosphere or mood, and connect with the target audience on a deeper level. By considering the personality of a typeface, designers can create more harmonious and engaging designs that resonate with the intended emotions and capture the essence of the message or brand.

Typeface Playfulness

Typeface playfulness refers to the visual characteristic of a typeface that conveys a sense of lightheartedness, whimsy, or creativity. It involves the use of unconventional design elements, such as exaggerated proportions, irregular shapes, and unique letterforms, to create a distinctive and playful appearance.

In the context of visual design and typography disciplines, typeface playfulness can be used to evoke specific emotions or communicate a specific message. Playful typefaces are often employed in designs aimed at younger audiences or to convey a sense of fun and informality. They can add a sense of character and personality to a design, making it more engaging and memorable.

Typeface Poster

A typeface poster is a visual design and typographic representation that showcases the characteristics and aesthetics of a particular typeface. It is an essential tool used by designers and typographers to communicate the unique features and qualities of a typeface to a specific audience or client.

A typeface, also known as a font, is a set of characters that share consistent design elements such as stroke width, serifs (or lack thereof), and overall style. Each typeface has its own personality, tone, and purpose, making it a vital part of visual communication and branding. Typeface posters are created to highlight these distinctive qualities.

The purpose of a typeface poster is to visually convey the essence and functionality of a typeface. It typically includes the name of the typeface, accompanied by carefully selected letters, words, or phrases that demonstrate its various characteristics. These examples showcase the typeface's legibility, readability, style, and versatility in different contexts.

Through the use of appropriate letterforms, spacing, scale, and colors, typeface posters provide designers and typographers with a detailed understanding of how the typeface can be effectively applied in different design projects. They allow designers to explore the visual potential of the typeface and determine how it aligns with their aesthetic preferences and design goals.

Typeface posters play a crucial role in typography disciplines as they inform the selection process and influence the overall visual impact of a design. They serve as a reference and source of inspiration, helping designers and typographers make informed decisions regarding the typography that best suits the intended message and target audience. Ultimately, typeface posters facilitate effective communication and enhance the overall visual experience through deliberate typeface choices.

Typeface Readability

Typeface readability refers to the ease with which a typeface can be read and understood by a reader. In the context of visual design and typography disciplines, readability holds paramount importance as it directly impacts the effectiveness of communication. A typeface that is difficult to read can hinder the transmission of information and create a negative user experience. On the other hand, a typeface that is highly readable enhances legibility and ensures that the intended message is effectively communicated.

Several factors contribute to the readability of a typeface, including the design of individual letters, spacing between letters and words, and overall legibility. The design of individual letters, such as the shape, proportion, and stroke thickness, plays a crucial role in determining readability. Additionally, the spacing between letters and words should be carefully considered to ensure clarity and prevent any confusion. Adequate spacing allows the reader's eye to move smoothly across the text, reducing the risk of misinterpretation or fatigue.

Typeface Rendering

Typeface rendering refers to the process of displaying or representing a typeface on a digital or printed medium. It involves converting the design of a typeface into an actual visual form that can be perceived and read by viewers. The rendering of typefaces is a crucial aspect of visual design and typography disciplines, as it directly affects the legibility, readability, and overall aesthetic appeal of a text.

When a typeface is rendered, various factors are taken into consideration to ensure its optimal display. These factors include the rendering method used, the resolution of the medium, and the specific characteristics of the typeface itself. Different rendering methods, such as anti-aliasing, subpixel rendering, and hinting, are employed to improve the clarity and smoothness of the rendered typeface. In visual design and typography, typeface rendering plays a significant role in determining the quality of the final typography.

A well-rendered typeface allows for easy reading and comprehension, enhances the visual hierarchy of a design, and contributes to the overall visual appeal of a composition. Conversely, poor rendering can result in distorted or jagged letterforms, leading to decreased legibility and negatively impacting the visual experience for readers.

Understanding typeface rendering is crucial for designers and typographers to create compelling and effective designs. By considering factors such as resolution, rendering methods, and the characteristics of the typeface, designers can ensure that their typography is presented in the best possible way, providing an optimal reading experience for viewers.

Typeface Selection

Typeface selection refers to the process of choosing the appropriate fonts or typefaces for a specific visual design or typography project. It is an essential aspect of design as it significantly impacts the overall aesthetic and readability of the text.

In the field of visual design, typeface selection involves considering various factors such as the purpose of the design, target audience, and the desired tone or mood. Different typefaces have their own unique characteristics, which can convey different emotions or messages.

For example, a bold and modern typeface may be more suitable for a contemporary and edgy design, while a classic and elegant typeface may be more appropriate for a traditional or formal design. Typography, on the other hand, focuses specifically on the arrangement and style of typefaces. When selecting a typeface, typographers consider factors such as legibility, hierarchy, and consistency.

Legibility refers to the readability of the typeface, ensuring that the text is easily readable and does not strain the reader's eyes. Hierarchy involves using different typefaces and sizes to establish a visual hierarchy and guide the reader's attention. Consistency refers to using a consistent set of typefaces throughout a design to create a cohesive and professional look.

The typeface selection process typically involves evaluating various typefaces, experimenting with different combinations, and considering how the typefaces will work in conjunction with other design elements. It requires a keen eye for detail, an understanding of typographic principles, and a deep knowledge of available typefaces. Overall, typeface selection plays a crucial role in visual design and typography disciplines, as it greatly influences the overall effectiveness and impact of a design. It requires careful consideration and a balance between aesthetics and functionality.

Typeface Style

A typeface style refers to a specific variation or variant of a typeface design. It encompasses the various attributes and characteristics of a typeface, such as its weight, width, slant or inclination, and optical size. Typeface styles are an essential component of visual design and typography disciplines as they allow designers to create visual hierarchy, establish tone and mood, and convey meaning through the written word.

In visual design, typeface styles are used to differentiate and categorize the various typefaces within a specific type family or system. For example, a typeface family may include regular, bold, italic, and condensed styles. Each style has its own distinct visual appearance, which can be applied to different design elements to create contrast or emphasis.

Typeface Tradition

Typeface Tradition refers to the historical and cultural background that influences the design and use of typefaces in the disciplines of Visual Design and Typography. It encompasses a wide range of traditional type design styles, techniques, and details that have been developed and passed down through generations of type designers.

Throughout history, different cultures and periods have shaped and influenced the development of typefaces. The characteristics of typefaces, such as letterforms, stroke widths, serifs, and ornamentation, have evolved over time. Typeface Tradition acknowledges and respects this evolution, honoring the legacy of classic typefaces while also embracing contemporary design trends.

Typeface Trend

A typeface trend refers to a specific style or design approach that becomes popular in the field of visual design and typography. It is a representation of the current preferences and aesthetic choices made by designers and typographers. Typeface trends can be influenced by various factors such as cultural shifts, technological advancements, and contemporary design movements. In visual design and typography disciplines, typeface trends play a crucial role in defining the character and visual appeal of a design. They serve as a means of visual communication and convey certain emotions, attitudes, and messages to the audience.

Typeface trends are not limited to individual characters or letters but encompass the overall style, proportion, weight, and spacing of a typeface. Designers and typographers often experiment with different typeface trends to create unique and visually engaging designs. They explore various styles such as minimalistic, vintage, hand-drawn, geometric, or experimental to evoke different moods and achieve specific design objectives. By following typeface trends, designers can create designs that feel contemporary and resonate with the target audience.

Typeface trends are constantly evolving, as new technologies and design practices emerge. Designers and typographers keep a close watch on the latest trends to stay relevant and create designs that align with the current aesthetic preferences. However, it's important to strike a balance between following trends and maintaining individuality in design. In conclusion, typeface trends are the prevailing styles and design approaches in the field of visual design and typography. They shape the visual character and mood of a design, allowing designers and typographers to create engaging and visually appealing compositions.

Typeface Usage

Typeface usage refers to the intentional selection and application of specific typefaces within visual design and typography disciplines. A typeface is a set of characters that share similar design features, such as the shape and style of the letters, numbers, and symbols. When it comes to typeface usage, designers must consider both aesthetic and functional factors.

The choice of typeface can greatly impact the overall tone and message conveyed by a design. Different typefaces have their own distinct personalities and associations. For example, a sans-serif typeface may be perceived as modern and minimalistic, while a serif typeface may be seen as more traditional and elegant. Designers must carefully select a typeface that aligns with the project's intended mood, audience, and brand identity. In addition to aesthetics, typeface usage also plays a crucial role in readability and legibility.

A well-chosen typeface should be easily readable at various sizes and distances. It should also be suitable for the intended medium or platform. For example, a typeface that works well in print may not translate effectively to a digital or mobile interface. Typography and visual design professionals must utilize their understanding of different typefaces, their characteristics, and best practices to make informed decisions when choosing and applying typefaces.

They must consider factors such as the hierarchy of information, contrast between different typefaces, and the overall composition of the design. Effective typeface usage not only enhances the visual appeal of a design but also helps to effectively convey and communicate information to the intended audience, making it an essential aspect of visual design and typography disciplines.

Typeface User Experience

Typeface User Experience refers to the overall satisfaction and effectiveness of using a specific typeface in a visual design or typography project. It encompasses the way a typeface communicates, its legibility, readability, and its ability to establish visual hierarchy and convey the intended message to the audience.

In visual design, typography plays a crucial role in organizing information, guiding the viewer's attention, and enhancing the visual appeal of the design. The typeface choice directly influences the user's experience by affecting readability and the perception of the design's tone and personality.

A well-designed typeface should align with the intended purpose of the design and effectively communicate the message. Legibility refers to the ease with which individual characters can be distinguished, while readability refers to the overall clarity and coherence of the text. Both legibility and readability are critical factors in delivering a positive user experience.

Visual hierarchy is another essential aspect of typeface user experience. It involves using different typefaces, sizes, weights, or styles to establish a clear order of importance and guide the reader's eye through the content. This allows the viewer to easily navigate and understand the information presented.

In conclusion, the typeface user experience is an integral part of visual design and typography. Choosing and implementing the right typeface can greatly impact how a design is perceived and understood by the audience. By prioritizing legibility, readability, and visual hierarchy, designers can create effective and user-friendly designs that successfully communicate their intended message.

Typeface Variation

Typface Variation refers to the different styles or designs of a typeface that are available within a font family. In the context of visual design and typography disciplines, typeface variation plays a vital role in creating visually appealing and effective designs.

Designers choose typeface variations based on the desired tone, mood, and message of the project. Typeface variations can range from subtle differences in weight, width, and style to more distinct variations such as bold, italic, condensed, or expanded versions. These variations allow designers to add emphasis, hierarchy, and contrast to the text, thereby enhancing the overall visual interest and readability of the design.

Typeface Versatility

Typeface versatility refers to the ability of a typeface to be used effectively across a range of applications and contexts in visual design and typography disciplines. It is a measure of how well a typeface adapts to different design requirements, such as varying sizes, mediums, and content types.

A versatile typeface is one that can maintain its legibility and visual appeal regardless of its size or medium. It should be equally effective when used for headlines, body text, captions, logos, or any other typographic element. A versatile typeface can also maintain its visual integrity and personality across different weights, styles, and variations.

Typeface Visuals

A typeface is a visual representation of a set of characters that share similar design features, such as stroke weight, proportions, and letterforms. It is an essential element in visual design and typography disciplines, as it contributes to the overall look and feel of a design or piece of written text.

In visual design, typefaces play a crucial role in conveying the intended message and setting the tone of a design. Different typefaces can evoke different emotions or communicate different themes, making the selection of an appropriate typeface critical to the success of a design. For example, a bold and geometric typeface may be used to convey a modern and minimalist aesthetic, while a decorative and handwritten typeface may be used to create a more playful and whimsical feel.

Typeface Web Design

Typeface Web Design refers to the process of selecting and implementing appropriate typefaces or fonts for designing websites. It is a crucial aspect of visual design and typography disciplines, as it directly affects the overall look and readability of a website. The choice of typeface can greatly influence the user experience, brand identity, and communication of the website's content.

When designing a website, designers must consider various factors such as the target audience, purpose of the website, and the overall design aesthetic. They need to select typefaces that align with the brand's personality and convey the desired message effectively. Typefaces can evoke emotions and set a certain tone, whether it's a formal, casual, elegant, or playful vibe.

Additionally, designers need to consider the readability and legibility of the chosen typefaces. The font size, spacing, and line height play a significant role in ensuring that the content is easily readable on different devices and screen sizes. A poorly chosen typeface can make the content difficult to read, leading to a negative user experience.

Furthermore, designers need to consider the compatibility of the chosen typefaces across various browsers and devices. The web design should be responsive and adapt to different platforms seamlessly. It is essential to test the typefaces on different browsers and devices to ensure consistency and optimal legibility.

In conclusion, Typeface Web Design is a critical aspect of visual design and typography disciplines, as it involves selecting and implementing appropriate typefaces to enhance the overall look, readability, and user experience of a website. It requires careful consideration of the target audience, brand identity, and readability factors to effectively convey the desired message and create a visually appealing design.

Typeface Weight

Typeface weight refers to the thickness or darkness of the characters in a typeface. It is an important attribute in visual design and typography as it plays a significant role in the overall appearance and legibility of a text.

The weight of a typeface is typically categorized into different font variations or styles, such as light, regular, bold, and black. Lighter weights are thinner and have less visual prominence, while heavier weights appear bolder and more commanding. Each weight can convey a different tone or mood, allowing designers to create visual hierarchy and convey emphasis within a text.

Typeface Whitespace

Typeface whitespace, also referred to as negative space, is an essential aspect of visual design within the realm of typography. It encompasses the unmarked areas surrounding and within typefaces, influencing the overall aesthetic and legibility of text. This form of whitespace is not to be confused with the conventional notion of blank or empty spaces; instead, it represents purposeful design choices that shape the experience of reading and comprehension.

Proper utilization of typeface whitespace is crucial in achieving visual balance and harmony. It allows for effective organization, guiding the viewer's attention, and emphasizing key elements. By strategically manipulating the spacing between letters, words, and paragraphs, designers can enhance readability, rhythm, and overall visual impact. Whitespace helps create a defined structure, preventing overcrowding and promoting a clear hierarchy of information.

Typeface Width

Typeface width refers to the relative thickness or thinness of the characters in a typeface. It is an essential attribute in visual design and typography that determines the impact and legibility of a text. The width of a typeface can vary from narrow to wide, and it plays a significant role in conveying the desired tone and style of a design.

In visual design, typeface width is a crucial element for creating visual hierarchy and establishing a clear typographic structure. Different widths can be utilized to distinguish headings, subheadings, and body text, allowing for a varied visual experience. Wide typefaces are often used for headlines or impactful statements as they tend to grab attention, while narrow typefaces are commonly employed for lengthy passages of text as they enhance legibility and readability.

Typography

Typography in the context of Design and User-Experience disciplines refers to the art and technique of arranging visual elements, primarily text, in a visually appealing and effective manner. It involves selecting and combining different typefaces, fonts, sizes, spacing, and alignment to enhance the readability, legibility, and overall aesthetic appeal of written content.

Typography plays a crucial role in conveying information, setting the tone, and establishing a brand identity in various design projects, such as websites, mobile apps, print materials, and digital interfaces. By carefully choosing and arranging typefaces, designers can create a hierarchy of information, guide users' attention, and evoke specific emotions or reactions.

Unity

Unity, in the context of Design and User Experience disciplines, refers to the principle of creating a sense of cohesion and harmony in a visual or interactive experience. It involves the seamless integration of various design elements and interactive features to form a unified and coherent whole.

Unity is achieved through careful consideration of various factors, such as balance, proportion, color harmony, and consistent use of typography and visual elements. It ensures that all the individual components of a design or user interface work together harmoniously, conveying a clear and consistent message to the user.

Visual Accessibility

Visual accessibility refers to the design and development of digital experiences that are inclusive and accessible to individuals with visual impairments or disabilities. In the context of design and user-experience disciplines, visual accessibility involves creating interfaces, content, and visual elements that can be easily perceived, understood, and navigated by all users, regardless of their visual abilities.

This includes considerations for individuals with various types of visual impairments, such as low vision, color blindness, and complete blindness. Designers and UX professionals must ensure that their websites or applications have clear and consistent layouts, readable text, and appropriate color contrast levels, making it easier for visually impaired users to interact with the digital content.

Visual Adaptability

In the context of design and user experience disciplines, visual adaptability refers to the ability of a design or interface to seamlessly adjust its appearance and layout across different screen sizes, resolutions, and orientations. It involves creating a design that is flexible and responsive, allowing it to be easily viewed and interacted with on various devices, such as desktop computers, tablets, and smartphones.

Visual adaptability is achieved through the use of responsive design techniques, which involve the use of fluid grids, flexible images, and media queries. By employing these techniques, a design can automatically adapt its layout and content to fit the screen it is being viewed on. This ensures that the design remains visually appealing and functional, regardless of the device or screen size.

Key considerations in achieving visual adaptability include:

- Responsive layouts that rearrange and resize content to fit different screen sizes

- Scalable and flexible images and media that adjust to various resolutions

- Consistent and accessible typography that is legible across different devices

- Optimized user interface components and interactions for touch-based devices

By designing with visual adaptability in mind, designers and user experience professionals can create a consistent and cohesive experience for users across different devices. The goal is to provide a seamless and optimized experience, allowing users to easily navigate and interact with the design or interface, regardless of the device they are using.

Overall, visual adaptability is a critical aspect of design and user experience, as it ensures that designs are accessible and usable across a wide range of devices and screen sizes.

Visual Adaptation

Visual adaptation is a concept used in design and user-experience disciplines to refer to the process of modifying the visual elements of a user interface or design to suit different devices, platforms, or user preferences. It involves making adjustments to the layout, typography, colors, and other visual elements in order to create a consistent and optimized experience across different screen sizes, resolutions, and display capabilities.

Visual adaptation plays a crucial role in ensuring that a design is visually appealing, functional, and accessible to a wide range of users. By adapting the visual elements, designers can create a seamless and enjoyable user experience regardless of the device or platform being used.

Visual Aesthetics

Visual aesthetics refers to the visual appeal and artistic qualities of a design or user experience. It encompasses various elements such as color, typography, layout, and imagery that are carefully designed to create a visually pleasing and harmonious experience for the user.

In the context of design, visual aesthetics play a crucial role in capturing the attention of users and making a lasting impression. A visually appealing design can elicit positive emotional responses, increase user engagement, and enhance usability. It helps to establish the brand identity and communicate the intended message effectively.

Visual Alignment

Visual alignment in the context of design and user experience disciplines refers to the intentional arrangement of visual elements on a page or screen to create a sense of order, hierarchy, and balance. It plays a crucial role in guiding the user's eye, improving readability, and enhancing the overall visual appeal of the design.

Alignment can be achieved through various techniques, such as using a grid system, aligning elements to a common baseline or axis, and creating equal spacing between elements.

These techniques help establish a visual connection between different elements and ensure that they are organized in a harmonious and cohesive manner. When visual elements are aligned properly, it creates a sense of visual balance and symmetry, making it easier for users to navigate and understand the content.

By using consistent alignment throughout a design, designers can create a clear visual hierarchy that highlights important information and guides the user's attention. Proper visual alignment not only improves the aesthetic appeal of a design but also contributes to its functionality and usability. It helps users quickly scan and digest information, reducing cognitive load and improving user comprehension.

By aligning elements in a logical and intuitive manner, designers can enhance the overall user experience and make the design more engaging and user-friendly. In conclusion, visual alignment is a critical aspect of design and user experience. By intentionally arranging visual elements in a cohesive and balanced manner, designers can create visually appealing, organized, and user-friendly designs that effectively communicate information and guide the user's attention.

Visual Analysis

Visual analysis refers to the systematic examination and interpretation of visual elements within a design or user experience. It involves evaluating various aspects of the visual presentation, such as color, typography, layout, and imagery, to understand how they contribute to the overall aesthetic appeal and usability of a product or interface.

This process involves breaking down the visual components into their individual parts and analyzing how they interact with each other and with the user. Designers and user experience professionals use visual analysis to assess how well the visual elements align with the intended goals and target audience of a product or interface.

Visual Arrangement

Visual arrangement in the context of design and user experience disciplines refers to the organization and placement of visual elements to create a cohesive and aesthetically pleasing design. A well-thought-out visual arrangement is crucial in design as it guides the user's eye, creates hierarchy, and helps communicate information effectively. It involves the strategic use of elements such as color, typography, imagery, composition, and space. Color plays a significant role in visual arrangement by creating contrast and attracting attention to key elements. It can be used to establish a visual hierarchy and indicate importance or relationships between different elements.

Typography, including font choice, size, and spacing, also contributes to the overall visual arrangement. It helps convey the mood, tone, and hierarchy in design. By using different font sizes, styles, and weights, designers can guide the user's eye to specific areas of the design. The composition of visual elements, such as their placement and alignment, affects how the user perceives and understands the design. It can create balance, rhythm, and harmony or intentionally disrupt these elements to create visual interest.

Understanding and implementing principles of composition, such as the rule of thirds or the golden ratio, can enhance the visual arrangement. Space, both positive (occupied) and negative (empty), is another essential component of visual arrangement. Proper spacing helps separate and group elements, improves readability, and creates a sense of visual balance. It also allows for easier navigation and interaction within a design. In conclusion, visual arrangement plays a vital role in design and user experience. By strategically organizing and placing visual elements, designers can create cohesive, visually pleasing, and effective designs that communicate information effectively and guide the user's eye.

Visual Asymmetry

Visual asymmetry, in the context of design and user-experience disciplines, refers to the intentional use of unequal or unbalanced elements to create a sense of visual interest, energy, and engagement within a design. It involves breaking away from perfectly symmetrical layouts and incorporating uneven distributions, different shapes, sizes, colors, or textures to create a dynamic and captivating composition.

This deliberate use of unevenness aims to draw the user's attention, evoke emotions, and guide their focus throughout the design. By introducing visual tension and disrupting the expected balance, visual asymmetry can make a design more engaging, memorable, and aesthetically appealing. It allows designers to create unique and artistic compositions that stand out from the crowd and convey a specific message or brand identity.

Visual Atmosphere

Visual atmosphere refers to the overall look, feel, and mood created by the visual elements of a design or user experience. It encompasses the combination of colors, typography, imagery, layout, and other visual elements that are carefully selected and arranged to convey a specific atmosphere or ambiance.

The visual atmosphere plays a crucial role in shaping the user's perception of a design or user experience. It has the power to evoke emotions, set the tone, and establish a certain aesthetic appeal. By carefully curating the visual elements, designers can create an atmosphere that aligns with the intended message, brand identity, or user expectations.

For example, a minimalist design approach with clean lines, muted colors, and ample white space can create a serene and calm visual atmosphere. This can be suitable for a meditation app that aims to promote relaxation and tranquility.

On the other hand, a bold and vibrant visual atmosphere with bright colors, dynamic typography, and energetic imagery can be more suitable for a fitness app that aims to inspire and motivate users.

In summary, visual atmosphere is a critical aspect of design and user-experience disciplines, as it sets the stage for how users perceive and interact with a product or service. By carefully considering and crafting the visual elements, designers can create a compelling and engaging atmosphere that enhances the overall user experience.

Visual Attraction

Visual Attraction is a concept within the disciplines of Design and User-Experience that refers to the ability of a visual element to capture and hold the attention of the viewer. It involves creating designs that are visually appealing and engaging, to effectively communicate information and elicit desired reactions from the user.

In the context of web design, visual attraction plays a crucial role in creating a positive user experience. When users visit a website, they form an immediate impression based on its visual design. If the design is visually attractive, users are more likely to engage with the content, explore the site further, and stay longer. On the other hand, if the design is unappealing or cluttered, users may quickly lose interest and navigate away from the site.

Visual attraction is achieved through various design elements, such as color, typography, imagery, layout, and overall aesthetic appeal. These elements should be thoughtfully combined to create a visually balanced and harmonious design that captures the viewer's attention and communicates the intended message effectively. Furthermore, the use of visual hierarchy and focal points helps guide the user's attention and ensures that important information or calls to action are easily noticeable.

In summary, visual attraction is a fundamental principle in design and user-experience disciplines. By creating visually appealing and engaging designs, designers can enhance the user experience, improve engagement, and communicate effectively with the target audience.

Visual Balance

Visual balance, in the context of design and user-experience disciplines, refers to the distribution of visual elements in a composition in a way that creates a sense of equilibrium and harmony. It is a fundamental principle that plays a crucial role in creating aesthetically pleasing and user-friendly designs across various mediums, including websites, applications, advertisements, and more.

Visual balance can be achieved by considering several factors, such as the size, color, and placement of elements within a design. There are two main types of visual balance: symmetrical and asymmetrical.

Symmetrical balance occurs when visual elements are evenly distributed on either side of a central axis, creating a mirror-like effect. This type of balance conveys a sense of stability, formality, and order. It is often used in formal designs and can help create a sense of reliability and trustworthiness.

Asymmetrical balance, on the other hand, involves the distribution of elements in an uneven manner. It relies on the visual weight of objects rather than their physical size or quantity. This type of balance creates a more dynamic and visually interesting composition. It is often used in modern and creative designs to evoke a sense of energy and movement.

Achieving visual balance is crucial in design and user experience as it can greatly impact how users perceive and interact with a product or interface. A well-balanced design ensures that important elements are easily identifiable and that the overall composition is visually appealing and harmonious. It helps users navigate and comprehend information more effectively, resulting in a more enjoyable and satisfying user experience.

Visual Clarity

Visual clarity is a fundamental aspect of design and user experience disciplines that refers to the ability of a visual element or interface to present information, content, and functionality in a clear and organized manner, allowing users to easily understand and navigate through the design.

Visual clarity involves the effective use of visual hierarchy, typography, color, spacing, and other design principles to create a visually appealing and intuitive design. It ensures that the intended message or purpose of the design is communicated clearly and effectively to the users. With visual clarity, users should be able to quickly and effortlessly identify and comprehend the information presented, locate desired elements or actions, and perform tasks without confusion or frustration.

Visual Closure

Visual Closure refers to the ability of a user to recognize or identify a whole object or pattern based on incomplete or partial visual information. In the context of Design and User-Experience (UX) disciplines, Visual Closure plays a significant role in ensuring effective and efficient communication between the user and the designed interface.

When users interact with digital interfaces, they often come across various elements and patterns that require their cognitive processing to complete the missing information. Designers leverage the concept of Visual Closure by providing users with visual cues and patterns that allow them to piece together the missing parts and comprehend the intended message or functionality.

Visual Cohesion

Visual cohesion is a fundamental principle in design and user-experience disciplines that refers to the harmonious integration and consistency of visual elements within a website, application, or any other designed interface. It is the key to ensuring a coherent and seamless experience for the users.

The concept encompasses various aspects, such as color, typography, layout, imagery, and overall visual language. Visual cohesion is achieved by establishing a clear visual hierarchy, using consistent styles and patterns, and maintaining a balanced composition throughout the design.

Visual Communication

Visual communication refers to the use of visual elements such as images, typography, and color to convey information and messages effectively. In the context of design and user experience disciplines, visual communication plays a crucial role in enhancing the overall user experience of a product or service.

Designers use visual communication to visually communicate their ideas, concepts, and designs to clients and stakeholders. By creating visual representations of their designs, designers can effectively convey their vision and ensure clear communication with others involved in the design process. Visual communication enables designers to express their creativity and design thinking in a visually appealing manner.

In the field of user experience, visual communication is instrumental in guiding users through digital interfaces and products. Through the use of visual elements such as icons, buttons, and navigation menus, users can easily understand the structure and functionality of a digital platform. Effective visual communication ensures that users can intuitively interact with the product and find the information or features they need without confusion or frustration.

Moreover, visual communication helps create a consistent and visually cohesive experience across different devices and platforms. By using consistent visual elements such as typography, color schemes, and branding elements, designers can establish a strong visual identity for a product or service, making it easily recognizable and memorable for users.

In conclusion, visual communication plays a vital role in design and user experience disciplines by visually conveying information, guiding users through interfaces, and creating cohesive and memorable experiences. It is an essential tool for designers and UX professionals in effectively communicating their ideas and enhancing the overall user experience.

Visual Complexity

Visual Complexity refers to the level of intricacy and intricacy present in a design or user experience. It assesses how visually demanding or intricate a design's structure, elements, and interactions are. Visual Complexity is a significant concept in design and user experience disciplines as it influences the user's perception, comprehension, and overall satisfaction.

A design with low visual complexity is characterized by simplicity, minimalism, and ease of understanding. It typically uses a limited number of elements, straightforward layouts, and clear communication. Low visual complexity designs are often preferred for tasks that require quick and efficient interaction, such as reading, scanning, or completing simple forms.

On the other hand, high visual complexity designs feature a greater number of elements, intricate patterns, and complex interactions. They often require more cognitive effort from the user to decode the information and navigate the design. High visual complexity designs can be beneficial for tasks that involve exploration, creativity, and extended engagement, such as immersive websites, data visualizations, or interactive games.

Designers and user experience professionals must carefully balance visual complexity to create optimal user experiences. It involves understanding the target audience, identifying usability requirements, and appropriately matching the level of complexity to the task at hand. By effectively managing visual complexity, designers can enhance user engagement, facilitate information processing, and ultimately improve overall satisfaction with the design or user experience.

Visual Composition

Visual composition in the context of Design and User-Experience disciplines refers to the arrangement and organization of visual elements within a design or interface. It involves the deliberate placement and manipulation of these elements to create an aesthetically pleasing and effective design that communicates the intended message or purpose.

Visual composition involves various principles and techniques, including balance, proportion, hierarchy, contrast, and rhythm. These principles help designers create harmonious and visually appealing compositions that guide the user's attention and enhance their overall experience.

Visual Connection

Visual Connection refers to the design principle that focuses on the relationship between elements in a composition in order to create a coherent and harmonious visual experience for the user. It involves the use of various design elements, such as color, shape, size, and alignment, to guide the user's attention and create a visual hierarchy.

In the context of design, visual connection plays a crucial role in enhancing user experience by making the content more visually appealing and easily digestible. By establishing visual connections between different elements, designers can create a sense of unity and cohesion, leading to a more engaging and intuitive user interface.

Visual Consistency

Visual consistency in the context of design and user experience disciplines refers to maintaining a cohesive and harmonious visual language throughout a product or system. It ensures that all visual elements, such as colors, typography, spacing, and layouts, are consistently applied across different pages, screens, or components. By maintaining visual consistency, designers aim to create a seamless and intuitive user experience, where users can easily understand and navigate through the interface. Consistency helps users develop mental models and expectations, allowing them to predict how certain elements or interactions will behave across different contexts.

Consistency can be achieved through various design principles and practices. One of the key aspects is using a consistent color palette to convey meaning and hierarchy consistently. Visual cues such as button styles, icons, and typographic treatments should also be used consistently to provide users with familiar and recognizable patterns. Layout consistency is another important factor in visual consistency. Designers should establish consistent grid systems or layout rules to maintain a clear visual hierarchy and structure.

Alignment, spacing, and placement of elements should follow these rules consistently throughout the design. Furthermore, visual consistency extends beyond the individual elements to the overall system. Different screens or pages should have a coherent and unified visual style, maintaining a sense of continuity. This includes consistent navigation patterns, information architecture, and overall branding elements. In conclusion, visual consistency is crucial in design and user experience disciplines to provide users with a predictable and cohesive visual experience. By maintaining consistency in color, typography, layout, and overall style, designers can enhance usability, trust, and overall satisfaction for the users.

Visual Continuity

Visual continuity refers to the consistent and seamless visual experience throughout a design or user experience. It encompasses the design elements such as color, typography, spacing, layout, and imagery, which are harmoniously integrated to create a cohesive and unified look and feel.

In the context of design and user-experience disciplines, visual continuity plays a crucial role in enhancing usability, aesthetic appeal, and brand recognition. It enables users to effortlessly navigate and interact with the interface, reducing cognitive load and improving overall user satisfaction.

Visual Contrast

Visual contrast is a design principle utilized in the fields of Design and User-Experience (UX) to create distinction and emphasis between elements within a composition or interface. It refers to the difference in visual properties such as color, size, shape, texture, and position, which allows users to easily differentiate and prioritize various elements.

By strategically using visual contrast, designers can guide users' attention and improve the overall usability and comprehension of a design. This principle is particularly important in UX design, as it helps users quickly grasp the hierarchy and relationships between different elements, ultimately enhancing their interaction and overall experience.

Visual Convergence

Visual Convergence refers to the strategic approach in design and user-experience disciplines that aims to bring different visual elements together to create a cohesive and harmonious user interface or experience. It involves the deliberate use of design principles, such as hierarchy, balance, contrast, and alignment, to guide the user's attention and provide a clear and intuitive visual organization.

By employing visual convergence, designers can create a seamless and unified interface that allows users to navigate and interact with the product or service more easily. The convergence of visuals helps reduce cognitive load by providing clear visual cues, making it easier for users to understand the information presented to them. This can greatly enhance the overall user experience, as users are able to quickly comprehend and make decisions or take actions within the interface.

Visual Creativity

Visual Creativity refers to the ability to generate unique and innovative visual solutions within the context of design and user experience disciplines. It involves the utilization of artistic skills, aesthetic judgment, and imagination to create visual elements that effectively communicate messages, engage users, and enhance the overall user experience.

Within the design field, visual creativity plays a crucial role in developing eye-catching and visually appealing designs that attract and captivate users. It involves the skillful combination of color, typography, imagery, and layout to create visually balanced and harmonious compositions. Visual creativity is essential in creating designs that stand out, leave a lasting impression, and differentiate a brand or product from its competitors.

In the realm of user experience, visual creativity focuses on creating visual elements that facilitate intuitive and meaningful interactions between users and digital interfaces. It involves the design of user interfaces that are aesthetically pleasing, visually coherent, and aligned with the brand's identity. Visual creativity improves user engagement and satisfaction by utilizing visually stimulating elements that guide users, provide feedback, and establish a sense of hierarchy and organization within the interface.

Visual creativity is not simply about aesthetics but also about effective communication and problem-solving. It requires a deep understanding of the target audience, the brand's objectives, and the overall user experience goals. By employing their imagination and artistic skills, designers can push boundaries, challenge conventions, and create visually compelling and memorable experiences that resonate with users and leave a lasting impact.

Visual Depth

Visual depth refers to the perception of distance and dimensionality in a design or user experience. It involves the use of various visual cues to create a sense of space, hierarchy, and realism.

In the context of design, visual depth is achieved through the manipulation of several design elements. One such element is the use of perspective, which allows objects to appear closer or farther away based on their position and size. Another important element is the concept of layers, where foreground and background elements are strategically placed to create a sense of depth and three-dimensionality.

Additionally, the use of shadows, gradients, and textures can also contribute to the perception of depth, as they provide visual clues about the surfaces and distances of objects within a design.

Visual Direction

Visual direction is a fundamental concept in the fields of design and user-experience disciplines. It refers to the process of guiding the visual elements of a design to create a cohesive and meaningful user experience.

This involves making intentional choices about various design elements such as color, typography, layout, imagery, and overall aesthetic to effectively communicate the intended message or purpose of the design.

The visual direction is derived from the project's objectives and target audience. It involves conducting research and analysis to gain an understanding of the user's needs, desires, and preferences. Based on this understanding, designers develop a visual direction that aligns with the brand identity and conveys the desired emotions or experiences.

Effective visual direction considers both functional and aesthetic aspects of design. It aims to create a visually appealing and engaging design that is also intuitive and easy to use. Consistency is a key principle in visual direction, ensuring that the design elements are coherent and cohesive throughout the user experience.

Additionally, the visual direction plays a vital role in establishing the hierarchy of information and guiding the user's eye flow. Through the strategic use of color, typography, and layout, designers can emphasize important elements, establish visual relationships between different elements, and create a clear and organized design structure.

Overall, visual direction is a critical aspect of design and user experience as it helps in creating a cohesive, visually compelling, and user-centric design that effectively communicates the intended message or purpose.

Visual Distinction

Visual Distinction refers to the use of various design elements and techniques to create clear and noticeable differences between different elements or components within a design or user interface. It plays a critical role in enhancing the user experience and guiding users' attention to important information or actions.

In the field of design, visual distinction helps to establish hierarchy and organize content by making certain elements stand out over others. This can be achieved through the use of contrasting colors, sizes, shapes, or typography. By creating visually distinct elements, designers can effectively communicate the importance and relationships between different parts of a design.

Visual Divergence

Using only two

tags:

Visual divergence refers to a design principle used in the disciplines of Design and User-Experience (UX) to create a distinct and visually appealing user interface. It focuses on the intentional deviation or differentiation from traditional design patterns or conventions to provide a unique and memorable user experience.

In Design and UX, visual divergence involves breaking away from standardized visual elements and layouts to create a fresh and engaging interface. It encompasses various aspects, including color schemes, typography, iconography, shapes, spacing, and overall composition. By diverging from established norms, designers can captivate users' attention and enhance their overall interaction with a digital product.

Visual Diversity

Visual Diversity in the context of Design and User-Experience disciplines refers to the practice of incorporating a wide range of visual elements to create a visually engaging and inclusive user interface.

By embracing visual diversity, designers aim to cater to the diverse needs and preferences of the user base. This involves incorporating various design elements such as colors, shapes, typography, images, and patterns to create an interface that is visually appealing, balanced, and inclusive.

Visual Dominance

Visual dominance, in the context of design and user experience disciplines, refers to the principle of using visual elements to direct and guide the user's attention within a design or interface. It is the ability of certain visual elements to stand out and capture the user's focus, effectively controlling the hierarchy of importance and creating a visual flow.

When applied appropriately, visual dominance plays a crucial role in enhancing the overall user experience by facilitating easy comprehension and efficient interaction. By strategically employing visual techniques such as color, size, contrast, and positioning, designers can guide users through a design, ensuring that important information or actionable elements are clearly seen and understood.

Visual Dynamics

Visual dynamics in the context of design and user-experience disciplines refers to the various visual elements and principles that contribute to the overall aesthetic appeal and user engagement of a design or digital interface. It encompasses the arrangement, movement, and interaction of these visual elements to create a visually compelling and effective user experience.

Visual dynamics include elements such as color, typography, imagery, layout, and spatial relationships. These elements are strategically combined and manipulated to evoke specific emotions, convey information, and guide user attention. The principles of visual dynamics, such as balance, contrast, repetition, and hierarchy, provide a framework for organizing and structuring these elements in a visually coherent and engaging way.

Visual Emotion

Visual Emotion refers to the psychological and physiological responses evoked in individuals through the visual aspects of design and user experience. It is a concept that encompasses the way people feel and perceive visual elements, such as colors, shapes, typography, and layout, when interacting with digital or physical products.

Within the field of design and user experience, visual emotion plays a crucial role in capturing users' attention, creating memorable experiences, and influencing their overall perception of a product or brand. By strategically using visual elements, designers can elicit specific emotions and reactions from users, ultimately enhancing their engagement and satisfaction.

Visual Emphasis

Visual emphasis is a design principle that is used in the disciplines of design and user experience to draw attention to specific elements or areas within a design. It involves making certain parts of a design stand out more prominently than others, thereby guiding the user's focus and enhancing the overall visual hierarchy. In design, visual emphasis is achieved through the strategic use of various visual elements such as color, size, contrast, and placement. By manipulating these elements, designers can highlight important information or actions that they want users to notice first. For example, using a bold and contrasting color for a call-to-action button can make it more visually prominent and increase the likelihood of user interaction. In the context of user experience, visual emphasis plays a crucial role in guiding users through a design and helping them understand the hierarchy of information. By emphasizing key elements, designers can effectively communicate the structure and importance of content within a user interface. This can improve user comprehension and navigation, as well as create a more engaging and intuitive user experience. Overall, visual emphasis is an essential tool in design and user experience disciplines to direct attention and create a visually appealing and functional design. By carefully considering how to draw attention to specific elements, designers can enhance usability, improve comprehension, and create a more engaging and memorable user experience.

Visual Engagement

Visual engagement refers to the effective and meaningful use of visual elements in design and user-experience disciplines. It encompasses the use of various visual elements such as images, colors, typography, and layout to capture the attention and engage the users in a specific design or user experience.

In the context of design, visual engagement is essential for creating visually appealing and aesthetically pleasing designs that attract and hold the user's attention. It involves the strategic placement of visual elements to guide the user's eye and create a visually cohesive and harmonious composition. The use of appropriate colors, typography, and imagery plays a vital role in evoking emotions, conveying information, and enhancing the overall user experience.

Similarly, in user-experience disciplines, visual engagement is crucial for creating user interfaces that are both visually appealing and easy to use. By using visual cues, such as icons, buttons, and other interactive elements, designers can guide users through the interface and provide them with a clear understanding of how to interact with the system. The use of visual hierarchy and consistency helps users prioritize information and navigate through the interface efficiently.

Overall, visual engagement is about creating designs and user experiences that captivate and connect with users on a visual level. It aims to enhance the overall usability, accessibility, and satisfaction by using visual elements purposefully and effectively. By understanding the principles of visual design and incorporating them into design and user-experience disciplines, designers can create engaging and memorable experiences for the users.

Visual Experience

The visual experience refers to the overall perception and interpretation of a design or user interface by an individual. It incorporates the visual elements such as color, shape, typography, and layout, as well as the overall aesthetics and harmony of the design. The visual experience is greatly influenced by the principles of visual design, including balance, contrast, proximity, alignment, and repetition.

In the context of design and user-experience disciplines, the visual experience plays a crucial role in creating a positive and engaging user interface. It aims to capture the attention of the user, convey information effectively, and evoke desired emotional responses. A well-designed visual experience can enhance usability, encourage user interaction, and reinforce brand identity.

Visual Exploration

Visual exploration in the context of design and user experience (UX) disciplines refers to the process of creatively and iteratively exploring different visual concepts and solutions to design challenges. It involves understanding the problem at hand, generating multiple ideas, and experimenting with various visual elements, such as color, typography, layout, and imagery. During visual exploration, designers aim to find the most effective and aesthetically pleasing ways to communicate their intended message or functionality to their intended audience.

They seek to create visual designs that are visually appealing, engaging, and intuitive to use. Visual exploration is an important part of the design process as it allows designers to brainstorm and generate a wide range of possible design solutions. By exploring multiple concepts, designers can compare and contrast different ideas, identifying strengths and weaknesses in each. This iterative process helps to refine and improve designs, enabling designers to make informed decisions based on user needs, preferences, and business goals. In UX design, visual exploration also plays a crucial role in creating an optimized user interface (UI) design. It helps designers to visualize how different visual elements work together to create a coherent and consistent user experience.

By exploring different visual concepts, designers can evaluate how these choices impact the usability, accessibility, and overall user satisfaction of a digital product or service. In summary, visual exploration is an iterative and creative process in design and UX disciplines, aiming to find the most effective and aesthetically pleasing visual solutions. It involves generating and evaluating multiple design concepts to optimize the user experience and effectively communicate the intended message or functionality.

Visual Expression

Visual expression refers to the use of visual elements such as color, typography, layout, imagery, and iconography to communicate and evoke emotions, set the mood, and convey information in design and user-experience disciplines.

Visual expression plays a crucial role in creating visually appealing and engaging experiences for users. It helps to establish a visual identity and personality for a brand, product, or interface. By carefully selecting and manipulating visual elements, designers can create an aesthetic that aligns with the goals and values of the project.

Visual Flow

Visual flow refers to the intentional and curated journey that a user takes when interacting with a design or user experience. It encompasses the arrangement and sequencing of elements, such as images, text, and interactive components, to create a cohesive and intuitive experience for the user.

Achieving effective visual flow involves several key considerations. Firstly, the layout and placement of elements should guide the user's attention and provide clear hierarchy. This can be achieved through the use of visual cues, such as size, color, and positioning, to draw focus to important elements and guide the user's eye through the desired path. Additionally, the use of whitespace and grouping helps to create visual relationships between related elements, aiding in the overall flow of the design.

Visual Focal Point

A visual focal point in the context of design and user-experience disciplines refers to a specific element or area within a design that captures the viewer's attention and directs their gaze. It is a strategic tool used by designers to guide users' visual flow and prioritize information or actions.

By creating a visual point of interest, designers can effectively communicate the hierarchy of content, guide user interactions, and enhance overall usability. The visual focal point can be achieved through various design techniques, such as contrast, size, color, and positioning.

Visual Focal Points

Visual focal points refer to specific elements within a design that capture the user's attention and guide their gaze or focus. They are strategically placed within the layout to attract and engage the user, improving the overall user experience.

In the context of design and user-experience disciplines, visual focal points play a crucial role in directing the user's attention and facilitating their understanding of the interface or content. These focal points are typically created using various design techniques such as contrast, size, color, positioning, and hierarchy.

Visual Fusion

Visual Fusion is a concept in the fields of Design and User-Experience that involves the integration and harmonization of various visual elements to create a cohesive and impactful experience for users. It is the art and science of combining different design elements such as color, typography, imagery, and layout in a way that not only pleases the eye but also communicates the intended message effectively.

At its core, Visual Fusion aims to create a visual hierarchy that guides users' attention and enhances their understanding and engagement with the content. Through deliberate and thoughtful arrangement of visual elements, designers can draw users' focus to the most important information or actions, while maintaining a consistent and unified visual language across different parts of a design.

Visual Grouping

Visual grouping refers to the arrangement and organization of elements in a design or user experience with the purpose of creating a sense of relatedness and cohesion. It involves the use of various visual cues, such as proximity, similarity, and continuity, to group together related elements and separate unrelated ones.

Proximity plays a significant role in visual grouping as elements that are physically close to each other are perceived as being more related. By placing related elements close together, designers create a visual cue that helps users group and process information more effectively. Similarly, the use of similarity, through color, shape, or size, can also aid in grouping elements. Users tend to perceive similar elements as being part of the same group, making it easier to navigate and understand the content.

Visual Harmony

Visual Harmony refers to the balanced and pleasing arrangement of visual elements in a design or user experience, resulting in a sense of unity and cohesion. It involves carefully considering factors such as color, shape, size, typography, and layout to achieve a harmonious and aesthetically pleasing composition.

Achieving visual harmony is essential in design and user experience disciplines as it enhances the overall appeal and effectiveness of the product or interface. When visual elements are harmoniously combined, they create a sense of order, clarity, and balance, making it easier for users to understand and interact with the design.

Visual Hierarchy

Visual hierarchy refers to the arrangement of elements in a design or user experience in a way that demonstrates their relative importance. It involves using visual cues to guide the viewer's attention and create a clear hierarchy of information.

The main goal of visual hierarchy is to make the design or user experience easy to understand and navigate by clearly indicating the importance of different elements. This can be achieved through the use of various design principles such as size, color, contrast, proximity, and typography.

Size is one of the most basic and effective ways to establish visual hierarchy. Larger elements tend to attract more attention and are perceived as more important. Color can also be used to differentiate and emphasize certain elements. Brighter or contrasting colors can draw attention to important information, while neutral or muted colors can make less important elements recede into the background.

Contrast plays a crucial role in visual hierarchy by creating a distinction between elements. Elements with high contrast, such as dark text on a light background, tend to stand out more and are perceived as more important. Proximity refers to the grouping of related elements together. Elements that are physically closer to each other are perceived as more related and should be given similar importance.

Typography is another important tool in establishing visual hierarchy. The use of different font sizes, weights, and styles can help differentiate between headings, subheadings, body text, and other types of content. Bold or italicized text can also be used to highlight important information within a block of text.

Visual Identity

Visual Identity is a concept within design and user-experience disciplines that refers to the overall look and feel of a brand or organization. It encompasses the visual elements, such as color, typography, imagery, and layout, that are consistently used to represent and distinguish the brand across various mediums.

A strong visual identity plays a crucial role in shaping the perception and recognition of a brand. It aims to create a cohesive and memorable experience for users or customers by conveying the brand's personality, values, and purpose. The visual elements are carefully chosen to evoke specific emotions or associations, and to effectively communicate the brand's message and identity.

Visual Impact

Visual Impact refers to the overall effect that a design or user experience has on the viewer or user. It encompasses the way in which design elements, such as color, typography, layout, and images, are combined to create a visually appealing and engaging experience.

In the context of design, visual impact is crucial as it determines the first impression and emotional response evoked by a design. A well-designed product or interface with strong visual impact immediately grabs the viewer's attention and communicates the brand's message effectively. It enables users to connect with the design on a deeper level, increasing their engagement and interest.

In the field of user experience, visual impact plays a vital role in enhancing usability and comprehension. A visually impactful interface assists users in quickly understanding the purpose and functionality of a product or website. It helps guide their interactions and provides visual cues, making the experience intuitive and enjoyable.

Designers and user experience professionals aim to create visual impact by carefully considering elements such as color theory, contrast, hierarchy, and balance. They use visual design principles to ensure that the layout, typography, and imagery work harmoniously together to create a cohesive and visually striking composition.

By prioritizing visual impact, designers and user experience professionals create designs that not only capture attention but also effectively communicate information and evoke positive emotions. A design with strong visual impact is memorable, engaging, and leaves a lasting impression on the viewer or user.

Visual Influence

Visual Influence refers to the impact and effect of visual elements on the perception, understanding, and behavior of users in design and user-experience (UX) disciplines. It encompasses the use of visual elements, such as color, typography, layout, and imagery, to communicate effectively, engage users, and create a compelling user experience.

In design, visual influence plays a crucial role in shaping the aesthetics and functionality of a product or interface. It involves the strategic use of visual elements to support the brand message, evoke emotions, and guide users through the design. Visual influence helps designers achieve visual hierarchy, where important elements stand out and grab users' attention, while less important ones are deemphasized. By carefully selecting and arranging visual elements, designers can create a visually coherent and intuitive design that enhances usability and user satisfaction.

In the field of UX, visual influence focuses on how visual elements contribute to the overall user experience. It recognizes that users interact with interfaces through visual perception and that their perception is influenced by various visual stimuli. Through visual influence, UX designers aim to create engaging and intuitive experiences that align with user expectations and needs. By using visual elements effectively, UX designers can guide users through tasks, promote discoverability, and enhance the overall usability of a product.

Overall, visual influence is a fundamental aspect of design and UX disciplines. It recognizes the power of visual elements to shape users' perception, understanding, and behavior. By leveraging visual influence, designers and UX professionals can create compelling and user-centered experiences that resonate with users.

Visual Innovation

Visual Innovation refers to the creation and implementation of unique and unconventional design solutions to enhance the user experience. It involves pushing the boundaries of traditional design principles to create visually captivating and engaging experiences for the end-user.

In the context of design, visual innovation goes beyond simply following established design conventions and trends. Instead, it challenges the status quo and embraces experimentation to create fresh and unexpected design solutions that captivate the user's attention. This can include the use of unconventional color schemes, typography, layout, and visual elements.

Visual innovation is closely tied to user experience (UX) design. By incorporating innovative visual elements into the overall user interface, designers can enhance the usability, accessibility, and overall enjoyment of the product or service. It helps to create a memorable and immersive experience for the user, encouraging them to engage and interact with the design in a meaningful way.

Through visual innovation, designers can evoke emotions, create brand recognition, and establish a unique identity for the product or service. It allows for differentiation in a crowded market and helps to leave a lasting impression on the user.

In conclusion, visual innovation plays a crucial role in design and user experience disciplines. By pushing boundaries and exploring new design approaches, designers can create captivating and engaging experiences that elevate the user's interaction with a product or service.

Visual Insight

Visual Insight refers to a concept in the fields of Design and User-Experience disciplines that focuses on the use of visual cues and elements to enhance the understanding and interpretation of information and data.

It involves the effective visual representation of complex data sets, allowing users to quickly and easily grasp the meaning and implications of the information presented.

Visual Insight utilizes various design principles and techniques, such as color, typography, layout, and visual hierarchy, to effectively communicate information in a visually appealing and meaningful way. Through the use of these elements, designers can create visualizations that aid in decision-making, problem-solving, and analysis.

By employing visual insight in their designs, designers are able to create intuitive and user-friendly interfaces that enable users to navigate through information with ease. Visual representations, such as graphs, charts, and interactive infographics, can enhance the user's understanding of complex concepts and make the information more accessible and engaging.

Furthermore, visual insight plays a key role in enhancing the overall user experience by reducing cognitive load and improving information comprehension. When users are presented with well-designed visualizations and engaging visual content, they are more likely to retain and assimilate the information being presented.

In conclusion, visual insight is an essential aspect of design and user experience, as it enables designers to effectively communicate complex information and enhance the overall user experience. By leveraging visual cues and elements, designers can create visually appealing and meaningful visualizations that aid in decision-making, problem-solving, and information comprehension.

Visual Integration

Visual integration refers to the process of seamlessly incorporating various design elements and visual components into a cohesive and harmonious user experience. It involves the deliberate and careful arrangement of visual elements, such as color, typography, images, and layout, to create a visually unified and balanced design.

In the context of design and user experience disciplines, visual integration plays a crucial role in enhancing the overall usability and aesthetic appeal of a product or service. By ensuring that all visual elements work together cohesively, visual integration helps to create a consistent and intuitive user interface.

When considering visual integration, designers must take into account both the individual design elements and their relationship to one another. Colors should complement each other and evoke the desired emotional response, typography should be legible and aligned with the brand's voice, images should reinforce the intended message, and layout should guide the user's eye and flow naturally.

The goal of visual integration is to create a visually pleasing and memorable experience for users. A well-integrated design not only attracts attention and engages users but also conveys credibility, professionalism, and trustworthiness. It helps to establish a strong visual identity and brand recognition.

In conclusion, visual integration is a critical aspect of design and user experience. By seamlessly combining various visual elements into a harmonious whole, designers can create aesthetically appealing, user-friendly, and memorable experiences that effectively communicate brand values and engage users.

Visual Intensity

Visual Intensity refers to the level of visual excitement or activity in a design or user experience. It is a measure of how much attention and focus is required from users when they interact with a visual element or interface.

In the context of design and user-experience disciplines, visual intensity plays a crucial role in capturing and maintaining users' attention. It can influence the overall impact, effectiveness, and user engagement of a design. By carefully controlling the level of visual intensity, designers can guide users towards desired actions or behaviors, and create more memorable and engaging experiences.

Visual Interaction

Visual Interaction is the design and execution of how users engage and interact with visual elements in a digital product or interface. It focuses on creating a fluid and intuitive visual experience that guides users through their interaction with the UI (User Interface) and enhances their overall user experience.

In the context of design and user experience disciplines, visual interaction encompasses various aspects. One key aspect is the use of visual cues and feedback to communicate the system's response to user actions. This includes visual indicators such as button states, hover effects, animated transitions, and real-time updates, which help users understand the outcome of their interactions and establish a sense of control and understanding.

Furthermore, visual interaction involves creating visually appealing and coherent interfaces that align with brand guidelines and engage users on an emotional level. It entails designing aesthetically pleasing layouts, colors, typography, and imagery that not only facilitate user interaction but also convey the brand's personality and values.

Effective visual interaction also considers the principles of visual hierarchy and organization to guide users' attention and facilitate their comprehension of the interface. This involves using contrast, spacing, and prioritization to highlight important information, guide users' navigation, and facilitate task completion.

Overall, visual interaction plays a vital role in creating a positive and engaging user experience. By leveraging visual elements and design principles, it enables users to easily and effectively interact with digital products and interfaces, enhancing their overall satisfaction and ensuring that their goals are met efficiently.

Visual Interest

Visual interest refers to the use of various design elements and techniques to captivate and engage the user's attention in the field of design and user-experience disciplines. It encompasses the arrangement, composition, and manipulation of visual elements to create a visually appealing and stimulating experience.

In the context of design, visual interest is achieved through the strategic use of colors, shapes, textures, patterns, and typography. By employing contrast, balance, hierarchy, and visual hierarchy, designers create a sense of harmony and dynamism that draws the user's eye to key elements, messages, or actions. Using these techniques, designers can guide the user's attention and create a visually engaging experience that enhances comprehension and interaction.

Visual Interpretation

A visual interpretation in the context of design and user-experience disciplines refers to the process of representing information or ideas through visual means, such as images, graphics, and typography. It involves using visual elements to convey meaning, evoke emotions, and enhance understanding.

The purpose of a visual interpretation is to communicate effectively with the target audience and create a visually appealing and engaging experience. It is an essential component of graphic design, web design, and user experience design, as it plays a crucial role in shaping how users perceive and interact with a product or service.

Visual Intuition

Visual Intuition refers to the ability to perceive and interpret visual elements in design and user-experience disciplines. It involves the understanding and skill to effectively communicate ideas and messages through visual means.

In design, visual intuition is crucial for creating visually appealing and engaging interfaces. Designers with strong visual intuition can make informed decisions about color, typography, layout, and visual hierarchy to ensure that the design conveys the intended message and elicits the desired emotional response from users. They can anticipate how users will interact with the design and make design choices that enhance usability and overall user experience.

Visual Mood

The visual mood refers to the overall atmosphere or feeling evoked by the visual elements and design choices in a particular design or user experience. It is determined by the composition, color palette, typography, imagery, and other visual elements used in the design.

In the context of design and user experience disciplines, creating the right visual mood is crucial in effectively communicating the intended message or brand identity and in eliciting specific emotional responses from the users. A well-crafted visual mood can enhance the user's engagement, build trust, and create a memorable and immersive experience.

The visual mood is achieved through careful consideration and harmonization of various design elements. The composition, or the arrangement of visual elements on the screen or page, plays a significant role in establishing the overall mood. Balanced and well-structured layouts can create a sense of stability and professionalism, while asymmetrical compositions may evoke a more dynamic or creative mood.

The color palette selected for the design also greatly influences the visual mood. Warm colors such as red and orange can evoke feelings of excitement or passion, while cool colors such as blue and green can create a sense of calmness or serenity. The saturation, brightness, and contrast of colors further contribute to the overall mood.

In addition, the choice of typography and imagery can reinforce the visual mood. Fonts with bold, strong, or elegant characteristics can convey different emotions and attributes. Similarly, the selection of relevant and meaningful imagery can contribute to the desired mood, whether it's by using photographs, illustrations, or abstract visuals.

Visual Movement

Visual Movement refers to the way elements in a design or on a user interface guide the viewer's eyes through a composition or layout. It involves using visual cues such as alignment, size, color, and contrast to create a sense of flow and direction, leading the user's attention from one element to another, and ultimately, to the desired focal point.

Visual Movement plays a significant role in enhancing the user experience by creating a seamless and intuitive navigation path. By strategically arranging elements and utilizing various design principles, designers can manipulate the viewer's gaze and direct it towards essential information or actions.

Visual Navigation

Visual Navigation refers to the process of guiding users through a digital interface by using visual cues and elements to help them understand the structure and hierarchy of the content. It plays a crucial role in the design and user-experience disciplines as it directly impacts how users engage with and navigate through a website or application.

Effective visual navigation aims to provide a clear and intuitive path for users to access the information they are seeking. It involves the use of various design elements such as menus, buttons, links, and icons, which are strategically placed and visually distinguishable to represent different sections or categories of content. By presenting these elements in a consistent and organized manner, users can quickly identify the available options and make informed decisions on where to go next.

Visual navigation also encompasses the use of visual hierarchy to prioritize and display content based on its importance or relevance. This can be achieved through the size, placement, and styling of different elements, ensuring that key information stands out and attracts users' attention. Additionally, it involves using appropriate labeling and descriptive text to provide clarity and context, reducing the need for users to rely solely on visual cues.

In summary, visual navigation is a fundamental aspect of design and user experience that utilizes visual cues and elements to guide users through a digital interface. It aims to create a seamless and intuitive navigation experience, enabling users to easily access the desired information and accomplish their goals within the digital environment.

Visual Noise

Visual noise, in the context of design and user-experience disciplines, refers to the presence of excessive or irrelevant visual elements that hinder the clarity, comprehension, and overall usability of a design or interface. It can be thought of as a form of unnecessary visual clutter that distracts and overwhelms users, making it difficult for them to focus on and extract meaningful information from a given design or interface.

Visual noise can take many forms, including but not limited to unnecessary graphics, excessive colors, inconsistent typography, overcrowded layouts, and excessive use of decorative elements. These elements can create a disorganized and chaotic visual experience, diminishing the overall effectiveness of the design and negatively impacting the user's ability to complete tasks efficiently.

Visual Order

Visual order refers to the arrangement of elements on a page in a way that guides users through the content in a logical and intuitive manner. In the context of design and user experience disciplines, visual order plays a crucial role in helping users understand, navigate, and interact with digital interfaces. The visual order is determined by various factors, including the placement, size, color, and contrast of elements. It is essential to establish a hierarchy of information, highlighting important elements and organizing content in a way that allows users to easily find what they are looking for.

Attention is a crucial aspect of visual order. By strategically placing elements that require immediate attention, such as call-to-action buttons or important messages, designers can guide users to take specific actions or draw their attention to specific information. Understanding the reading pattern of users is also essential in establishing visual order. Most users scan content in an F-shaped pattern, starting at the top left and moving horizontally, with fewer fixations as they move down the page.

Designers can leverage this knowledge by placing important information and headlines at the top and left of the page, making it more likely to grab users' attention. Additionally, visual order helps in creating a sense of visual hierarchy. By using size, color, contrast, and whitespace effectively, designers can differentiate between different levels of importance or relatedness, ensuring that users can easily distinguish between primary and secondary content.

Overall, visual order in design and user experience disciplines is about creating a visually appealing and well-organized interface that facilitates easy comprehension, navigation, and interaction for users. Through the careful arrangement of elements and consideration of user behavior and patterns, designers can guide users through the content and enhance the overall user experience.

Visual Path

A visual path is a key concept within the design and user-experience disciplines that refers to the predefined sequence in which visual elements are presented to guide users' attention and facilitate their understanding of information within a design or interface.

The visual path encompasses the arrangement and hierarchy of visual elements such as text, images, and interactive elements within a design. It ensures that important information is easily noticeable and effectively communicates the intended message to users.

By strategically organizing and presenting visual elements, designers can direct users' attention to specific areas of a layout while helping them navigate and comprehend the content effectively.

Visual Pattern

A visual pattern refers to the recurring arrangement, motif, or design element used in the creation of a digital interface or user experience. It serves as a guideline or template that ensures consistency and coherence across different parts of a design. In the context of design disciplines such as graphic design and user experience (UX), visual patterns help in organizing and structuring information, guiding users' interactions, and enhancing the overall visual appeal.

These patterns can be applied to various elements within a design, including navigation menus, buttons, typography, color schemes, iconography, and layouts. Visual patterns play a crucial role in UX design by providing users with familiar and intuitive interactions.

They decrease cognitive load by allowing users to recognize and understand design elements quickly, enabling them to navigate through the interface effortlessly. Moreover, consistent visual patterns across an application or website help establish a sense of trust and reliability, as users can predict how certain elements will behave based on previous experiences. Designers create visual patterns by following established design principles, industry best practices, and user research findings.

They aim to strike a balance between creativity and conventionality, ensuring that the patterns are aesthetically pleasing, functional, and aligned with the users' needs and expectations. By leveraging visual patterns, designers can create cohesive and user-friendly interfaces that promote positive user experiences.

Consistency in the visual elements and interactions not only enhances the usability of a product but also contributes to brand recognition and differentiation. In summary, visual patterns serve as design guidelines that ensure consistency, familiarity, and usability within digital interfaces. They provide users with intuitive interactions, decrease cognitive load, and establish trust in the product or brand.

Visual Patterns

Visual patterns in the context of design and user-experience disciplines refer to recurring visual elements or design motifs that are used consistently throughout a design system or user interface to create a cohesive and consistent visual language. These patterns are designed to enhance usability, improve user experience, and communicate effectively with the users.

Visual patterns can include elements such as buttons, icons, typography, color schemes, layout grids, and imagery styles. These patterns help users understand and navigate through different sections of a website or application, providing familiarity and predictability. By using consistent visual patterns, designers can ensure that users have a seamless and intuitive experience across various screens and interactions.

Visual patterns also contribute to brand recognition and differentiation. By incorporating unique visual elements into the patterns, designers can create a distinct visual identity for a product or service, making it easily recognizable and memorable for the users.

In order to create effective visual patterns, designers need to consider various factors such as accessibility, responsiveness, and scalability. Visual patterns should be accessible to users with different abilities and should adapt to various devices and screen sizes.

Additionally, they should be scalable to accommodate future design iterations and updates. Overall, visual patterns play a crucial role in enhancing the overall user experience by providing consistency, usability, and brand recognition. They are an essential design tool for creating visually appealing and effective user interfaces.

Visual Perception

Visual perception refers to the cognitive process and interpretation of visual information by an individual. It involves the reception, organization, and understanding of visual stimuli through the senses, enabling individuals to make sense of their surroundings.

In the context of design and user-experience disciplines, visual perception is of utmost importance. Designers strive to create visually appealing and functional interfaces that effectively communicate information to users. By understanding how users perceive visual elements, designers can make informed decisions in crafting user interfaces that are intuitive and engaging.

Visual Perspective

Visual perspective refers to the way an object or scene is visually represented, conveying depth, scale, and spatial relationships. In the context of design and user experience disciplines, visual perspective plays a crucial role in creating realistic and visually pleasing digital experiences.

By utilizing visual perspective techniques, designers can provide users with a sense of depth and dimension, allowing them to navigate and interact with digital interfaces more intuitively. This can be achieved through the use of various visual cues, such as shading, gradients, and perspective grids, to create the illusion of three-dimensional space on a two-dimensional screen.

Visual Proportion

Visual proportion in the context of design and user-experience disciplines refers to the relative size and relationship of elements within a composition. It governs the arrangement and distribution of objects, shapes, and text on a page or screen.

Proportion plays a crucial role in creating balance, harmony, and visual appeal in design. It helps guide the viewer's gaze, create hierarchy, and communicate messages effectively. By applying proper visual proportions, designers can influence how users perceive and navigate through digital interfaces, websites, and products.

Visual Proximity

Visual proximity is a fundamental principle in the field of design and user experience (UX) that refers to the placement of related elements in close physical or visual proximity to each other. It is based on the idea that items that are grouped together are perceived as being more closely related or connected than those that are spaced further apart.

By organizing elements that are visually similar or conceptually related in close proximity, visual proximity helps to create a visual hierarchy, guide users' attention, and improve overall usability. It allows users to quickly and intuitively understand the relationship between different elements and helps to reduce cognitive load by making it easier to process information.

Visual Readability

Visual readability refers to the ease with which text and other visual elements can be read and understood by users. It is an important aspect of design and user-experience disciplines, as it directly impacts the user's ability to consume and comprehend information efficiently.

Visual readability is influenced by various factors, including font choice, font size, line length, line spacing, and contrast. Choosing a legible font and the appropriate font size ensures that text is easily readable for users.

It is important to select fonts that have distinct letterforms and clear differentiation between uppercase and lowercase letters.

The length of lines of text can also impact visual readability. Lines that are too long can make it difficult for users to track and follow the text. Conversely, lines that are too short can create unnecessary breaks in reading flow. Optimal line length allows users to read comfortably without getting lost or losing their place.

Line spacing, or leading, plays a crucial role in visual readability. Sufficient spacing between lines ensures that text is not cramped together, making it easier for users to distinguish between lines and move their eyes smoothly across the content.

Lastly, contrast between text and its background is essential for visual readability. High contrast helps maintain legibility, especially for users with visual impairments. It is important to choose colors that provide enough contrast to ensure the text stands out clearly against the background.

Visual Reflection

Visual reflection in the context of design and user experience disciplines is the process of critically analyzing and evaluating the visual aspects of a design or user interface to gain insights and improve its effectiveness. It involves carefully examining the visual elements such as colors, typography, layout, imagery, and overall aesthetics to assess their impact on the user experience and the intended message or functionality of the design.

Visual reflection aims to uncover how the design choices influence the user's perception, emotions, and behavior. By analyzing the visual composition, designers can identify strengths, weaknesses, and areas where improvements can be made to enhance the overall user experience. This process often involves comparing the design against established design principles and best practices to ensure that it meets design objectives and effectively communicates the intended message.

Visual Relationship

Visual relationship refers to the arrangement, placement, and connection of visual elements within a design or user experience. It involves the intentional organization of these elements to create a cohesive and harmonious composition that effectively communicates information and engages the user.

In the context of design, visual relationship encompasses various principles, such as balance, proximity, alignment, and contrast. These principles guide the designer in establishing a systematic and structured arrangement of elements that convey hierarchy, group related information, and establish a clear flow of visual communication.

Effective visual relationship enhances the user experience by facilitating easy comprehension, smooth navigation, and efficient interaction. Through the strategic arrangement of visual elements, users can quickly and intuitively understand the content, find desired information, and complete tasks with ease.

Furthermore, visual relationship plays a crucial role in establishing brand identity and personality. Consistent use of visual elements, such as color schemes, typography, and graphic styles, helps build recognition and reinforce brand attributes in the minds of users.

Overall, visual relationship is essential in design and user experience disciplines as it determines the overall coherence, functionality, and aesthetic appeal of a product or interface. By skillfully arranging visual elements, designers can create meaningful and engaging experiences that effectively convey information, guide users, and reinforce brand identity.

Visual Repetition

Visual Repetition refers to the deliberate use of recurring visual elements or patterns in a design or user experience to create a sense of consistency, cohesiveness, and familiarity. This design principle is often employed to enhance visual organization, improve readability, and establish a visual rhythm.

In design, visual repetition can be achieved through various techniques, such as repeating colors, shapes, lines, textures, or imagery. By repeating these elements throughout the design, a sense of unity and harmony is created. This repetition helps users navigate the interface more easily and understand the underlying structure of the design.

Visual repetition is an essential tool in user experience design, as it aids in establishing familiarity and predictability. Consistent visual cues and patterns allow users to quickly recognize and understand the functionality of different elements and interactions. When elements repeat in a consistent manner, users can build mental models and develop expectations, which in turn reduces cognitive load and improves usability.

By employing visual repetition, designers can create a cohesive and memorable aesthetic. When users encounter familiar visual elements or patterns throughout an interface, they feel a sense of unity and coherence. This can contribute to a positive user experience and help reinforce brand identity.

In summary, visual repetition is a design principle that involves the deliberate repetition of visual elements or patterns to establish consistency, improve readability, and enhance the overall user experience. It aids in organizing information, reducing cognitive load, and creating a cohesive and memorable design aesthetic.

Visual Representation

Visual representation is a fundamental concept in the disciplines of Design and User-Experience. It refers to the use of graphical elements such as images, charts, diagrams, and typography to convey information, communicate ideas, and enhance the overall user experience.

In the context of Design, visual representation plays a crucial role in creating and communicating the intended message or concept. It allows designers to showcase their ideas, solutions, and designs in a visually appealing and understandable manner. Visual representations help designers capture the attention of the audience, convey the design intent effectively, and provide a clear visual hierarchy that guides the user's attention through the design elements.

Similarly, in the realm of User-Experience, visual representation is essential for creating intuitive and user-friendly interfaces. It aids in facilitating users' understanding of the system, guiding them through different tasks, and providing visual feedback. Visual representations in UX design help in creating meaningful and memorable experiences, ensuring that users can easily comprehend and interact with the interface elements.

By utilizing visual elements strategically, designers can enhance the overall usability, appeal, and effectiveness of the designs. Visual representation allows designers and UX professionals to simplify complex information, highlight key features, establish a consistent visual language, and elicit specific emotions or responses from the user.

Visual Resonance

Visual Resonance refers to the harmonious and impactful relationship between visual elements in a design, resulting in a compelling and memorable user experience. It encompasses the effective use of color, typography, layout, and imagery to evoke an emotional response and establish a coherent visual language.

Within the context of design and user-experience disciplines, visual resonance plays a crucial role in capturing and retaining users' attention, facilitating information absorption, and conveying the intended message. By utilizing consistent design principles, such as balance, proximity, contrast, and hierarchy, designers aim to create visual resonance that enhances the overall aesthetic appeal and usability of a product or interface.

Visual Response

Visual Response is a fundamental concept in the disciplines of Design and User Experience (UX) that involves communicating information, emotions, and messages through visual elements in a deliberate and intentional way. It encompasses various elements such as color, typography, imagery, layout, and graphics to shape the visual language of a product or service.

In the context of Design, Visual Response refers to the visual aesthetics and overall presentation of a design. It involves creating a visually appealing and cohesive experience that resonates with the user's expectations, preferences, and cultural background. By carefully selecting and combining visual elements, designers aim to evoke specific emotions, establish brand identity, and enhance usability and comprehension.

In the realm of User Experience, Visual Response takes into account how users perceive and interact with visual stimuli. It focuses on designing user interfaces that are visually engaging, intuitive, and facilitate efficient and enjoyable user interactions. A visually effective interface can help users understand the structure and hierarchy of content, guide them through different tasks, and provide visual feedback to their actions.

Visual Response plays a crucial role in capturing and holding users' attention, conveying information effectively, and establishing a strong visual identity for a brand or product. By utilizing visual design principles and understanding the psychological impact of visual elements, designers can create visually compelling experiences that resonate with users and convey messages or information in an engaging manner.

Visual Restraint

Visual Restraint is a design principle that promotes simplicity and minimalism in the visual presentation of a user interface. It involves using a limited color palette, reducing the number of visual elements, and prioritizing clarity and ease of use.

By employing Visual Restraint, designers aim to create a clean and uncluttered visual experience that enhances the overall user experience. This principle emphasizes the importance of removing any unnecessary or distracting elements that could overwhelm or confuse the user. It encourages designers to focus on the essential elements and functionality of the interface, ensuring that they are easily understood and accessible.

Visual Rhythm

Visual rhythm in design and user-experience disciplines refers to the intentional arrangement of visual elements to create a sense of movement, harmony, and coherence within a layout or interface. It is the repetition and variation of visual elements, such as colors, shapes, lines, and textures, that establish a rhythmical pattern and guide the viewer's eye through the design.

Visual rhythm plays a crucial role in enhancing the user's understanding and engagement with the content. When applied effectively, it helps to create a visual hierarchy, prioritize information, and improve the overall readability and usability of a design or interface. By establishing a rhythm, a sense of order and predictability is achieved, which allows the user to navigate and interact with the interface more intuitively.

Visual Sensation

Visual sensation refers to the perception and interpretation of visual stimuli by the human visual system. In the context of design and user experience disciplines, visual sensation plays a crucial role in how users perceive and interact with digital products and interfaces.

Designers leverage visual sensation to create visually appealing and aesthetically pleasing designs that attract and engage users. By understanding how the human visual system processes and perceives visual information, designers can strategically use colors, shapes, textures, and other visual elements to elicit specific emotional reactions and guide users' attention to important information or actions.

Visual Simplicity

Visual Simplicity in the context of Design and User-Experience disciplines refers to a minimalistic approach to aesthetics and presentation. It involves the deliberate use of clean and uncluttered design elements, with a focus on removing unnecessary visual distractions and complexities.

By adopting visual simplicity, designers aim to create a clear and intuitive user interface that enhances usability and overall user experience. It involves reducing visual noise, using a limited color palette, employing whitespace effectively, and adhering to a consistent visual hierarchy.

Visual Space

Visual space refers to the arrangement and presentation of visual elements within a design or user experience. It encompasses the spatial organization and distribution of these elements, such as images, text, icons, and interactive elements, on a screen or any other visual medium.

In the context of design, visual space plays a crucial role in conveying information, establishing hierarchy, and guiding user attention. It involves the use of principles like balance, proportion, contrast, and alignment to create a visually pleasing and effective composition. Designers strategically manipulate visual space to emphasize certain elements, create focal points, or establish relationships between different components of a design.

Within the realm of user experience, visual space directly influences how users perceive and interact with digital interfaces. It helps in guiding users' focus, reducing cognitive load, and improving overall usability. By effectively using visual space, designers can make interfaces more intuitive and user-friendly, ensuring that users can easily find and understand the information they need.

By carefully considering the visual space, designers can create a harmonious and visually appealing experience that engages users and effectively communicates the desired message. It involves understanding the relationship between different elements, maximizing the use of available space, and leveraging techniques like whitespace and grouping to create clear and organized designs.

Visual Stimulation

Visual stimulation refers to the use of visual elements, such as colors, shapes, and patterns, in design and user-experience disciplines to engage and captivate individuals visually. It involves the strategic arrangement of these elements to create a visually appealing and stimulating experience for users.

In design, visual stimulation plays a crucial role in capturing users' attention and guiding them through the intended user journey. By employing visual techniques, designers are able to communicate messages effectively, evoke emotional responses, and enhance the overall user experience.

Color is a fundamental visual element that can evoke specific emotions and convey different meanings. The careful selection and combination of colors can evoke specific moods or feelings, and create a visually cohesive and aesthetically pleasing design. Similarly, the use of shapes and patterns can help communicate branding, hierarchy, and visual flow within a design, enabling users to interact with the interface intuitively.

Visual stimulation is closely tied to the principles of visual hierarchy, balance, and rhythm. Designers utilize these principles to organize elements in a visually pleasing manner, structuring information and directing users' attention to the most important or relevant content. This enables users to navigate easily and efficiently through the design.

Overall, visual stimulation is a fundamental aspect of design and user-experience disciplines. It encompasses the strategic use of visual elements, such as colors, shapes, and patterns, to engage users, evoke emotions, communicate messages, and enhance the overall user experience.

Visual Storytelling

Visual storytelling in the context of design and user experience disciplines refers to the practice of using visual elements, such as images, graphics, and typography, to convey a narrative or message. It is a method of communication that engages and captivates users by combining visual and textual components to create a cohesive and compelling story.

Through visual storytelling, designers and UX professionals aim to enhance the user's understanding and engagement with a product, service, or brand. By strategically arranging and presenting visual elements, they can guide the user's attention, convey emotions, and communicate information effectively.

Visual Structure

Visual structure refers to the arrangement and organization of visual elements in a design or user experience. It encompasses the way visual elements are laid out, grouped, and related to each other to create an overall composition. In design disciplines such as graphic design, visual structure plays a crucial role in communicating information effectively and creating a visually appealing design.

It involves determining the hierarchy and arrangement of elements such as images, text, colors, and shapes to guide the viewer's attention and facilitate understanding. In the context of user experience design, visual structure is vital for creating intuitive and user-friendly interfaces. It helps users navigate and interact with digital products by providing clear pathways and visual cues.

Effective visual structure ensures that key information and actions are easily discoverable and promotes a seamless user experience. Visual structure can be achieved through various design principles and techniques, such as:

1. Balance: Distributing visual weight evenly to create a sense of equilibrium and harmony.

2. Proximity: Grouping related elements together to establish visual relationships and enhance comprehension.

3. Alignment: Ensuring that elements are aligned along a consistent axis to create a sense of order and structure.

4. Contrast: Highlighting differences between elements to make important information stand out and create visual interest.

5. Repetition: Repeating visual elements, such as colors or shapes, to create a cohesive and unified design.

6. Grid systems: Using a grid as a framework to align and organize elements on a layout, ensuring consistency and coherency.

By employing these design principles, designers can establish an effective visual structure that enhances both the aesthetics and usability of a design or user experience.

Visual Surprise

Visual Surprise refers to an unexpected or unique element incorporated into a design or user-experience that captures the attention and creates a sense of intrigue or delight for the user. It is a strategic approach used by designers and user-experience professionals to engage and enthrall users by going beyond their anticipated expectations.

In the disciplines of Design and User-Experience, Visual Surprise plays a significant role in enhancing the overall usability and appeal of a product or service. By incorporating unexpected or visually stimulating elements, designers can create memorable experiences that leave a lasting impression on users.

Visual Symmetry

Visual symmetry, in the context of design and user-experience disciplines, refers to a balanced composition where the elements on one side of a central axis mirror or replicate the elements on the other side. It is a fundamental principle in graphic design, aiming to create harmony, order, and a sense of equilibrium within a layout or interface.

By using visual symmetry, designers can guide the user's attention, establish hierarchy, and enhance the overall aesthetic appeal of a design. Symmetrical compositions are often perceived as stable, elegant, and organized, providing a sense of familiarity and reassurance to the user.

Visual Synthesis

Visual Synthesis is a process in design and user-experience disciplines that involves the consolidation and organization of visual elements and information to create a cohesive and meaningful visual representation. It is the practice of visually synthesizing complex concepts, data, or ideas into a simplified and easily digestible format.

Through visual synthesis, designers and user-experience professionals aim to present information in a visually compelling and engaging manner, facilitating understanding and communication. It involves the thoughtful arrangement of visual elements such as images, icons, typography, and colors to create visual hierarchies, emphasize key messages, and guide the user's attention. In the design process, visual synthesis plays a crucial role in creating intuitive and user-friendly interfaces. It helps to distill complex user scenarios and requirements into clear and accessible visual representations.

By visually synthesizing user research, personas, and user flows, designers can gain a deeper understanding of user needs and effectively communicate design solutions. Similarly, in the field of user experience, visual synthesis is employed to analyze and make sense of user feedback, behavior patterns, and analytics data. It enables designers to identify trends and insights that inform iterative design improvements.

Overall, visual synthesis is an essential skill in the design and user-experience disciplines as it aids in simplifying complex information, enhancing communication, and creating impactful and visually appealing designs.

Visual Texture

Visual texture refers to the perceived surface quality or tactile feel of an object or element in a design. It is a design principle that focuses on creating the illusion of texture through visual stimuli, without any actual physical texture being present. In the context of design and user-experience disciplines, visual texture plays a crucial role in enhancing the overall aesthetic appeal and usability of a design.

Visual texture can be achieved through various design elements, such as color, pattern, and shape. By strategically incorporating these elements, designers can simulate different surface qualities, such as roughness, smoothness, or coarseness, to evoke specific emotions or convey a particular message. For example, using a rough texture in a design may invoke a sense of ruggedness or authenticity, while a smooth texture may communicate sleekness or elegance.

Visual Transformation

Visual transformation refers to the process of changing the visual appearance or design of a product or interface in order to enhance the user experience and improve the overall functionality and aesthetics. It involves modifying the look and feel of a design element, such as the color scheme, typography, layout, and visual elements, to create a more visually appealing and engaging user interface (UI) or user experience (UX).

In the context of design, visual transformation is a crucial aspect as it helps in creating a strong brand identity and establishing a consistent and memorable visual language. By carefully considering the target audience and their preferences, designers can transform the visual elements to evoke specific emotions and establish a connection with the users.

Visual Transition

A visual transition in the context of design and user experience disciplines refers to the method of smoothly changing one visual element to another. It is commonly used to enhance the user's understanding of changes happening on a website or application, providing them with a clear visual cue.

This technique is particularly useful during the process of interaction design, where the transition can help users perceive changes in the interface more easily. By employing visual transitions, designers can guide users' attention and make the overall experience more intuitive and engaging.

Visual Unity

Visual Unity refers to the design principle that focuses on creating a cohesive and harmonious visual experience in a given design or user-experience (UX).

In the context of design disciplines, Visual Unity involves the arrangement and organization of visual elements such as shapes, colors, typography, images, and spatial relationships to create a sense of coherence and balance. It aims to ensure that all the elements in a design work together seamlessly and convey a clear and consistent message to the audience.

In UX design, Visual Unity plays a crucial role in providing users with a cohesive and intuitive experience. It involves consistent use of colors, typography, and visual elements across different screens and interactions within a digital product or website. Visual Unity helps users easily navigate and understand the interface, ensuring a smooth and enjoyable user experience.

By maintaining Visual Unity, designers can create a visually pleasing and aesthetically pleasing design that enhances user engagement and satisfaction. It helps establish brand identity, sets the tone and mood, and reinforces important information or actions within a design or UX context.

To achieve Visual Unity, designers pay attention to factors such as proximity, alignment, contrast, and hierarchy. These principles help create a visual hierarchy that guides the user's attention, clarifies information, and emphasizes important elements.

In conclusion, Visual Unity is an important design principle that fosters coherence and consistency in both visual design and user-experience disciplines. It ensures that the elements within a design work together harmoniously, resulting in a more engaging and effective design or UX experience.

Visual Variation

Visual variation refers to the deliberate use of diverse visual elements in design and user experience to create interest, hierarchy, and differentiation.

In the field of design and user experience, visual variation plays a crucial role in effectively communicating information, guiding users, and establishing a unique brand identity. By employing a range of visual attributes such as color, shape, size, texture, and typography, designers can evoke specific emotions, emphasize important content, and create a visually engaging experience.

Visual Weight

Visual weight is a concept used in design and user-experience disciplines to describe the perceived heaviness or prominence of elements within a design composition. It refers to the visual impact or significance that different elements convey to the viewer's eye.

Visual weight is influenced by various factors such as size, color, contrast, and positioning. Larger and more prominent elements tend to have greater visual weight compared to smaller or less pronounced elements. Similarly, elements with bold or vivid colors, high contrast, or unique shapes tend to attract more attention and carry more visual weight than elements that are more muted or blend into the background.

Visual Whitespace

Visual whitespace, in the context of design and user experience disciplines, refers to the intentional use of empty space within a layout or design to improve clarity, organization, and overall visual appeal. It is the absence of any visual elements or content in a specific area.

Also known as negative space, visual whitespace contributes to the readability and comprehension of a design by providing separation between elements, reducing clutter, and enhancing focus on the key information. It allows the eye to rest and helps establish a hierarchy of content, guiding users' attention to the most important elements on the page.

The strategic placement and size of visual whitespace greatly impact the overall balance and harmony of a design. It can be used to create an elegant and sophisticated aesthetic, as well as to communicate a sense of modernity and simplicity.

By incorporating visual whitespace effectively, designers can improve the user's experience by making it easier for them to navigate, find information, and engage with the content. It can create a sense of spaciousness and cleanliness, giving users a feeling of ease and comfort while interacting with the interface or layout.

Visual whitespace is a powerful tool that designers use to not only enhance the aesthetics but also improve the functionality and usability of a design. It is a fundamental principle in design, guiding the placement of elements and content to create a visually pleasing and user-friendly experience.

Warm and Cool Colors

Warm and cool colors are terms used in the fields of design and user experience to describe two different color palettes that have distinct psychological and emotional effects on the viewer.

Warm colors refer to the hues that are associated with fire, sunlight, and warmth. These colors include red, orange, and yellow. Warm colors are often used to create a sense of energy, excitement, and positivity. They can evoke feelings of warmth, passion, and enthusiasm.

Cool colors, on the other hand, are associated with water, the sky, and cooler temperatures. These colors include blue, green, and purple. Cool colors are often used to create a sense of calmness, serenity, and relaxation. They can evoke feelings of tranquility, peace, and stability.

In the context of design, warm colors are often used to grab attention and create a focal point. They can be effective in drawing the viewer's eye and creating a sense of urgency or importance. Cool colors, on the other hand, are often used to create a more soothing and harmonious visual experience. They can be effective in creating a sense of balance and reducing stress.

In the field of user experience, warm colors are often used to communicate action, such as buttons or links, as they can create a sense of urgency and encourage interaction. Cool colors, on the other hand, are often used to communicate information or provide a sense of calmness and clarity to the user.

White Space

The term "white space" refers to the empty areas or gaps in a design or user interface that are intentionally left blank or unoccupied. It is a crucial element in design and user experience disciplines as it helps create a visually appealing and functional layout.

White space allows for better organization, readability, and comprehension by providing breathing room between different elements or sections of a design. It helps to separate and distinguish different elements, such as text, images, icons, or buttons, making them more digestible and easier to understand.

By strategically using white space, designers can prioritize important elements, guide users' attention, and create a more balanced composition. It helps in reducing visual clutter and cognitive load, enhancing the overall user experience.

White space can be both active and passive. Active white space refers to intentionally placing empty areas between elements to create a specific visual or functional effect. Passive white space occurs naturally due to the placement of elements, margins, or gaps between lines of text.

When used correctly, white space can improve legibility, highlight important content, enhance user engagement, and create a sense of elegance and sophistication. It plays a vital role in promoting ease of use and user satisfaction by making designs more intuitive and user-friendly.

In conclusion, white space is an essential design element that contributes to the overall aesthetics, usability, and readability of a design or user interface. It acts as a visual separator, organizes content, and enhances the overall user experience.

Whitespace Balance

Whitespace balance refers to the intentional distribution of blank space within a design to create a harmonious visual composition and enhance user experience. In the context of design and user experience disciplines, whitespace, also known as negative space, is the area around and between design elements.

A well-balanced use of whitespace in a design allows for better legibility, organization, and focus. It provides visual breathing room and allows the user to comprehend information more easily. By properly allocating whitespace, designers can guide the user's attention to key elements or content. Whitespace can be categorized into two types: macro and micro.

Macro whitespace refers to larger empty areas, such as margins, gutters, and spacing between major sections. This type of whitespace aids in providing structure and separation between different blocks of information. On the other hand, micro whitespace is the smaller space between individual elements like paragraphs, buttons, or icons. Micro whitespace helps to create visual clarity and establish relationships between the elements.

Achieving whitespace balance requires careful consideration and decision-making. Designers need to strategically determine the appropriate amount of whitespace for different components, depending on their importance and hierarchy. It involves finding the right equilibrium between too much or too little whitespace to optimize the user's experience.

By implementing proper whitespace balance, designers can effectively enhance readability, draw attention to important information, and evoke a sense of elegance and simplicity. It contributes to a visually clean and organized design, allowing users to navigate, comprehend, and engage with the content effortlessly. Overall, whitespace balance plays a significant role in creating visually appealing and user-friendly designs by leveraging the power of empty space to guide and enhance the user experience.

Whitespace Economy

Whitespace Economy refers to the intentional use of empty or blank spaces in the design and user-experience disciplines. It involves strategically incorporating white or negative spaces within a layout or interface to enhance the overall user experience and visual appeal.

In design, whitespace serves as a powerful tool to create balance, increase readability, and improve the user's perception of a website or application. It allows important elements, such as text, images, or buttons, to stand out and be easily comprehensible. By introducing breathing room around content, whitespace helps prevent information overload and provides a sense of visual hierarchy.

In the context of user experience, whitespace plays a crucial role in guiding users' attention and interaction. It enables users to focus on essential elements, navigate through the interface effortlessly, and understand the content more effectively. Furthermore, it contributes to the overall usability and accessibility of a design by making it accessible to a wider range of devices and resolutions.

Whitespace Economy is not mere blank space but rather a strategic approach to design that requires thoughtful consideration. It entails understanding the context, purpose, and goals of a project and using whitespace as a deliberate design element to enhance clarity, simplicity, and user engagement.

Whitespace Emphasis

Whitespace emphasis is a design principle used in the disciplines of Design and User-Experience (UX). It involves the strategic use of empty space, typically in the form of margins, padding, and line breaks, to create a visual hierarchy and draw attention to the content and elements that are most important. Whitespace emphasis is a fundamental aspect of good design as it enhances the readability, usability, and overall aesthetic appeal of digital interfaces and printed materials.

By incorporating whitespace, designers can effectively guide the user's focus and navigation, improving the user experience and helping to convey the intended message or purpose of the design. Whitespace emphasis helps to prevent clutter and overwhelming visual elements and allows the user to digest information in a more organized and efficient manner. It helps to define boundaries between different sections and elements, allowing for clear content grouping and reducing cognitive load.

Through careful consideration of whitespace, designers can achieve balance and harmony in their designs, ensuring that the user's attention is directed to key information and functionality. It allows for proper contrast and separation between elements and enhances the overall aesthetic, making the design more visually appealing. In summary, whitespace emphasis is an essential design principle in the disciplines of Design and User-Experience that involves the intentional use of empty space to create visual hierarchy, enhance readability, and improve the overall user experience.

By strategically incorporating whitespace, designers can guide the user's focus and create a more balanced and aesthetically pleasing design.

Whitespace Hierarchy

In the context of design and user-experience disciplines, whitespace hierarchy refers to the deliberate use of empty space or negative space to create a visual structure and hierarchy within a design. Whitespace, also known as negative space, is the space between elements in a layout that is left intentionally empty. It can be in the form of margins, padding, or gaps between paragraphs, images, and other elements.

Whitespace hierarchy plays a crucial role in guiding the user's attention, emphasizing important elements, and improving readability and comprehension. By strategically utilizing whitespace, designers can create a clear and organized visual hierarchy that helps users understand the content and navigate through the interface more easily. It allows the eyes to rest, separates different sections or blocks of information, and provides a sense of visual balance.

Whitespace Utilization

Whitespace utilization refers to the intentional and strategic use of empty space within a design or user experience in order to enhance its overall effectiveness. Also known as negative space, whitespace refers to the areas in a layout that are left intentionally empty or devoid of any visual or textual elements.

Whitespace utilization plays a crucial role in design and user experience disciplines as it impacts the overall balance, readability, and clarity of a design. When utilized effectively, whitespace can improve the user's ability to comprehend and interact with the content on a website or in an application.